Jacob of Sarug's Homily on the Creation of Adam and the Resurrection of the Dead

Texts from Christian Late Antiquity

37

Series Editor

George Anton Kiraz

TeCLA (Texts from Christian Late Antiquity) is a series presenting ancient Christian texts both in their original languages and with accompanying contemporary English translations.

Jacob of Sarug's Homily on the Creation of Adam and the Resurrection of the Dead

Translation and Introduction by

Edward G. Mathews Jr.

gorgias press
2014

Gorgias Press LLC, 954 River Road, Piscataway, NJ, 08854, USA

www.gorgiaspress.com

Copyright © 2014 by Gorgias Press LLC

All rights reserved under International and Pan-American Copyright Conventions. No part of this publication may be reproduced, stored in a retrieval system or transmitted in any form or by any means, electronic, mechanical, photocopying, recording, scanning or otherwise without the prior written permission of Gorgias Press LLC.

2014

ISBN 978-1-4632-0264-4

ISSN 1935-6846

Library of Congress Cataloging-in-Publication Data

```
Jacob, of Serug, 451-521.
  [D-'al bríteh d-'Adam w-hayat míte. English]
  Jacob of Sarug's Homily on the Creation of
Adam and the resurrection of the Dead /
translation and introduction by Edward G.
Matthews Jr.
       pages cm. --  (Texts from Christian late
antiquity, ISSN 1935-6846)
   In English and the original Syriac.
   Includes bibliographical references.
   ISBN 978-1-4632-0264-4
  1.  Theological anthropology--Christianity. 2.
Adam (Biblical figure) 3.  Resurrection.  I.
Matthews, Edward G., Jr., 1954- II. Title.
   BR65.J283D3 2014
   233'.1--dc23

2014009185
```

Printed in the United States of America

TABLE OF CONTENTS

Table of Contents v
Abbreviations vii
Introduction 1
   Outline 1
Notes on the Text 9
   Title 9
   Manuscripts 9
   Summary 11
Text and Translation 13
   Jacob of Sarug 14
   Mêmrâ 72: On the Creation of Adam and the Resurrection of the Dead 14
   I. Adam was the pinnacle and culmination of all beauty of creation 14
   II. The demise of Adam and the dissolution of his composition 20
   III. The purpose of every detail of Adam's constitution 26
   IV. Adam and Eve adorned in garments of light; extinguished by the Evil One 30
   V. The Son came down to restore Adam's lost image 34
   VI. The second coming, the new creation and the end of the old 38
   VII. The new creation will be one of unending light 42
   VIII. The end of the world is death and dissolution 46
   IX. An exhortation to forsake temporal things and look to the eternal 50
   X. Adam will rise up again at the general resurrection 52
   XI. The spiritual nature of the new creation 54
   XII. The same Adam will rise up and regain his garment of light 56

Bibliography of Works Cited 61
    Primary Texts 61
        Ephrem 61
        Gregory of Nyssa 61
        Isaac [of Antioch] 61
        Jacob of Sarug 62
        Narsai 62
        Theodore of Mopsuestia 62
    Secondary Works 62
Index 65
    Names and Themes 65
    Biblical References 66

ABBREVIATIONS

Alwan	K. Alwan, *Jacques de Saroug, Quatre Homélies métriques sur la Création* (see Bibliography)
Bedjan	P. Bedjan, *Homiliae Selectae Mar-Jacobi Sarugensis* (see Bibliography)
BETL	Bibliotheca Ephemeridum Theologicarum Lovaniensium
BUSE	Bibliothèque de l'Université Saint-Esprit
CBOTS	Coniectanea Biblica. Old Testament Series
CSCO	Corpus Scriptorum Christianorum Orientalium
CSS	Cistercian Studies Series
FOTC	Fathers of the Church
OCP	*Orientalia Christiana Periodica*
OS	*L'Orient Syrien*
OtSt	*Oudtestamentische Studien*
PdO	*Parole de l'Orient*
PO	Patrologia Orientalis
SC	Sources Chrétiennes
TFCLA	Texts from Christian Late Antiquity

INTRODUCTION

> INFORMATION ON THIS HOMILY
> Homily Title: On the Creation of Adam and the Resurrection of the Dead
> Source of Text: *Homiliae Selectae Mar-Jacobi Sarugensis*, edited by Paul Bedjan (Paris-Leipzig: Harrassowitz, 1907, 2nd ed. Piscataway: Gorgias Press, 2006), vol. 3, pp. 152–175 [Homily 72]; *Jacques de Saroug, Quatre Homélies métriques sur la création*, edited by Khalil Alwan, (CSCO 509; Louvain: Peeters, 1989) 78–105. [Homily 4]
> Lines: 454 [+12]

OUTLINE

The *Mêmrâ* "On the Creation of Adam and on the Resurrection of the Dead", numbered 72 in the edition of the works of Jacob of Sarug published by Paul Bedjan, follows immediately the *Mêmrâ* "On the Days of Creation" in that same edition.[1] *Mêmrâ*, or *Homily*, 72 is a meditation on the fall of Adam and the consequences of that fall for him, for humanity and even for the entire world. This *mêmrâ* does indeed follow — thematically as well as textually — his long seven-part *Mêmrâ* "On the Days of Creation", but this leaves the reader of Bedjan's edition of Jacob's *Homilies* a bit perplexed nonetheless, as to why Jacob seems to jump right over the text of the fall itself into this meditation on its aftermath.

---

[1] Cf. Bedjan, III.1–151; the precise title of this homily is "On the Fashioning (Syr. *tûqōnô*) of Creation". An English translation of the first section of this homily regarding day one has appeared in E.G. Mathews, Jr., *Jacob of Sarug's Homilies on the Six Days of Creation: The First Day*. The remaining sections of this long homily will also soon appear in separate fascicles in the same series.

It has long been known from the various manuscript catalogues that Jacob did in fact compose more *mêmrê* on this subject than Bedjan had included in his *Homiliae Selectae*. It is even more fortunate that these additional homilies that are pertinent to the homily translated here can now be found in modern critical texts with accompanying annotated French translations. Just over a quarter century ago now, Fr. Khalil Alwan published a more critical edition of Homily 72, along with three other previously unedited homilies concerning the figure of Adam. The four *mêmrê* included in this edition are the following:

a. On the verse, "Come, let us make man in our own image after our likeness";

b. Was Adam created mortal or immortal?;

c. On the Expulsion of Adam from Paradise;

d. On the Constitution of Adam (= Homily 72).[2]

Clearly these four homilies, when taken together with *Mêmrê* 71, "Homily on the Days of Creation" present a much more complete picture of Jacob's thought on the biblical text of Genesis 1–3, and they fill in an important gap that had existed in our knowledge of Jacob's theology of creation.

It is to be noted that within this small group of four homilies, we seem to have examples of two different genres of exegesis. Philippe Gignoux first noticed the same combination of expository genres in the works of Narsai and labelled them "commentary proper", "free commentary" and "doctrinal exposition". The four works of Jacob under consideration here seem to fall into the first: a. and c.; and third: b. and d.; of these categories.[3] That we have such examples from both Jacob and Narsai on the creation accounts, and specifically on the subject of Adam, suggests that we may have here vestigial evidence of how similarly exegesis of the bible was taught at the School of Edessa and its offshoot the

---

[2] K. Alwan, ed. and tr., *Jacques de Saroug Quatre homélies métriques sur la création*. On the difference in the title of this homily, see further, below.

[3] P. Gignoux, *Homélies de Narsaï sur la création*, 12–14.

School of Nisibis, despite how much they differ on a number of theological positions.[4]

In point of fact, these four homilies also seem to serve as witness to Jacob's contribution to a much wider discussion on the nature of Adam, a discussion that was prevalent not only in the West, but very much so in the East as well.[5] The Council of Chalcedon, which took place around the time of Jacob's birth, clearly did not solve the issue of the identity of Christ as it had intended, but discussion also became acute over the precise nature of the first Adam as well. It has already been shown how the question of whether Adam was created mortal or immortal was a particularly acute one between proponents of the School of Edessa and its fledgling offshoot, the School of Persia, led in the beginning by Jacob's arch-antagonist Narsai.[6] As one would expect, Jacob here tended to follow the exegesis of Ephrem as opposed to Narsai who, as was his wont tended to side with the exegesis of Theodore of Mopsuestia.

The homily printed and translated here begins (ll. 1–14) with two central, but contrasting, facts. Following the general patristic interpretation of Genesis 1–2,[7] Jacob makes Adam the pinnacle of God's creation, a "god of flesh"[8] who was set on the summit of Paradise, and to whom all of Paradise was given save one single tree. Due to his own weakness, however, he listened to the deceptive guile of the serpent and turned his back on God and ate from

---

[4] For a recent study on the general curriculum of the latter, see A.H. Becker, *Fear of God and the Beginning of Wisdom*.

[5] For some of these ideas in areas west of Syria, see P. Bouteneff, *Beginnings*, passim.

[6] See K. Alwan, "L'homme était-il mortel ou immortel avant le péché, pour Jacques de Saroug", and L. Van Rompay, "Humanity's Sin in Paradise: Ephrem, Jacob of Sarug, and Narsai in Conversation".

[7] For a preliminary sketch of this theme in early Syriac writers, see E.G. Mathews, Jr., "'What Manner of Man?': Early Syriac Reflections on Adam."

[8] See translation, below, line 3, and note ad loc.

that one forbidden tree, thus incurring an incalculably huge fall from that pinnacle, from the highest height to the lowest depth.[9]

Jacob then turns to just how great the creation of Adam actually was (ll. 15–50). Adam was not the pinnacle only because he was created the highest of God's creatures, but even more so because in him were constituted "all the colors that are in natures" and in whom were set "all natures, both those endowed with senses and those that are not". "All beauties of all creatures were culminated in [Adam]". Following nearly every other early Christian writer, Jacob sets Adam as an intermediary between heaven and earth. He was the great image of God through which God and His wisdom were made manifest to the rest of creation.

Jacob then proceeds to a long, detailed description of the greatness of Adam's creation and the power and wisdom of God in bringing it about (ll. 51–110). Who else would be capable of combining all these disparate elements into a single corpus? Who else would be able to harness opposites, such as heavy and light or hot and cold, within a single body? Such is the image of God; only it can proclaim how glorious, how marvelous, how powerful, and how omnipotent its Creator is.

God formed Adam (ll. 111–192) with eyes to gaze on his fellow creatures, feet that he might go to visit them, hands that he might feel and caress them, mouth and nostrils to discern tastes and smells, hearing and speech, and of course his brain as a most fitting receptacle for his mind. But the serpent, in his envy and rebelliousness, came and induced Adam to cast all this aside. Adam and Eve lost the garment of light in which they had been created, and they stood naked before all of creation. Adam's constitution was then dissolved, but as all creation was embodied in him so too the rest of creation also began to decompose; all the disparate elements that God had brought into harmony began to separate and to disperse. Not only did "all creation groan in travail (Rom 8:22)" but it fell and came to naught.

---

[9] On this theme in early Syriac literature, see L. Van Rompay, "Humanity's Sin in Paradise: Ephrem, Jacob of Serugh, and Narsai in Conversation".

But the Son of the Great King departed His heavenly realms and came down to restore His image that had become corrupted (ll. 193–236). He who was even higher than Adam descended into those very same depths that Adam had fallen into in order to bring him, and thus all creation, back to the place that had been promised to him. Here Jacob proposes a three-fold schema of salvation history, each of which is grounded in God's mercy (or compassion)[10] for humanity: creation, redemption and resurrection. Jacob himself summarizes this schema as follows:

> In mercy He formed him, in mercy He delivered him from robbers,
> and in mercy He will come again at the end and raise him back up.
> …
> thus, in a three-fold way, He finishes him, makes him whole, and perfects him.

This will all come to pass at the second coming which will cause all creation to tremble and quake, and be marked by the various hosts of heaven accompanying Him: angels, Apostles, holy ones and faithful ones (ll. 237–316). At this time all that had become corrupted and dissolved will be restored and refashioned in a brand new way, one that will not require light or movement; since Christ will eclipse all other lights there will be no further need for the sun or moon, their rising or setting, or their courses. There will be no east or west quadrants for the sun to traverse through, no morning or evening; Christ will be the sole source of light, the Sun of Righteousness.

The world as it was known will disappear (ll. 317–378). So that it can be easily perceived, its death will resemble the death of a human body; the sun and moon will go dark like human pupils, etc. Jacob then enters into an exhortation to the reader to recognize these signs and to break off any and all attachments to this world

---

[10] In this homily, Jacob uses the Syriac term *raḥmê* for God's mercy/compassion, but elsewhere he uses other synonymous terms; see T. Kollamparampil, *Salvation in Christ according to Jacob of Serugh*, 195–196.

and its fleeting pleasures, for it is heading to a complete and total end.

But at that end, while the world dissolves, Adam will rise up and inherit that treasure that was promised to him from the beginning (ll. 379–454). Jacob here resumes several of the images: the voice, the trembling, etc., that he had previously invoked to describe the end of days, the dissolution of this world, while he puts greater emphasis on the fact that while creation is falling, Adam will rise up. At this time, his body will be renewed and become incorrupt, perfect and immortal. While Jacob asserts that this body will be the very same one as the original (l. 440), it will now move in a spiritual fashion and will "pass through even solid natures" (l. 420), and be reclothed in light.

Jacob's purpose in composing this "doctrinal composition" is less clear than in his *Mêmrâ* "Was Adam created mortal or immortal?". He certainly wants to emphasize the final resurrection, as well as God's mercy that had watched over Adam from the beginning and that had ensured that Adam was indeed granted that treasure he had been promised from the beginning – his immortality. Whereas the world was created and then decomposed, Adam, and therefore humanity, rose up in spiritual bodies that were both the same yet also new. From Jacob's presentation here in *Mêmrâ* 72 of God's great mercy and from what he says elsewhere in his homilies,[11] Jacob seems to imply that his three-fold schema for Adam was God's plan from the beginning; there was no change in this plan after Adam and Eve ate from the tree of knowledge,[12] for God has done nothing that He did not have planned from the very beginning.[13] In any case, this is a subject that deserves much deeper

---

[11] See, especially, Jacob's *Mêmrâ* "On the verse, 'Come, let us make man in our own image after our likeness'", Alwan I.33–54.

[12] Pace L. Van Rompay, "Humanity's Sin in Paradise: Ephrem, Jacob of Serugh, and Narsai in Conversation", 209–211. Compare T. Kollamparampil, "Adam-Christ Complementar[it]y," 156–159, and idem., *Salvation in Christ according to Jacob of Serugh*, 203–209.

[13] See Jacob's *Mêmrâ* "On the verse, 'Come, let us make man in our own image after our likeness'", Alwan I.48.

investigation than can be given in this short introduction to a single homily.

NOTES ON THE TEXT

TITLE

In his critical edition and translation of this *mêmrâ* Alwan prefers the shorter alternate title as found in Br. Lib. Ms. Syr. 12162: "On the Constitution of Adam". This title, while it is from the oldest of the three manuscripts, describes only a portion of the text of this *mêmrâ*, whereas the more traditional title, maintained here, captures better the subject matter of the entire *mêmrâ*. This is corroborated by the words of Jacob himself who almost certainly refers to this *mêmrâ* when he says in his *Mêmrâ*, "*On the Expulsion of Adam from Paradise*":

> I speak here briefly of Adam's expulsion,
> when necessary I will speak of his return.
> …
> I sing now of [Adam]'s expulsion from Paradise
> but I am reserving some verses that will address his return.
> The Lord did not create him to leave Paradise,
> but to enter there and be its heir and ruler.[1]

MANUSCRIPTS

Bedjan consulted two manuscripts in his edition of Jacob's *Mêmrâ* 72: Ms. Oxford Syr. 135 (now Pocock 404) and Ms. London (now British Library) Syr. 12162. As he noted in his introduction, he did not necessarily include all the variants from the London manuscript.[2] In his new critical edition of 1989 for the Louvain series CSCO, Khalil Alwan also consulted Ms. Vat. Syr. 117, which offers

---

[1] Alwan, III.163–164, 167–170.
[2] Bedjan, III.x.

a number of different readings from the edition as printed in Bedjan. In addition, Alwan also referenced the Arabic and Ethiopic versions of this homily, which were never consulted by Bedjan.

As the focus of this series is to translate the text as found in Bedjan (and most of these variants do not significantly alter the meaning of this *mêmrâ*, anyway) I have refrained from cluttering up this volume by taking note of all the Syriac variants found in Alwan's edition, much less the additions/variants found in the Arabic and Ethiopic versions. I have, however, taken Alwan's edition into account in two instances. I have added one line, l. 60, directly into the text translated below. It is likely that this line was omitted in Bedjan's text simply by accidental omission, but since it is clearly required by the parallelism of lines I have simply inserted it into the text where it belongs. There are also twelve additional lines from Ms. Vat. Syr. 117 that Alwan includes in his edition but which are not found at all in the edition of Bedjan. These twelve lines, which simply expand the image Jacob was painting at the pertinent juncture of his *mêmrâ*, are provided here — in the original Syriac and in translation — for the sake of completeness; they would fall between lines 246 and 247 of the text and translation found below:

ܝܡܐ ܕܢܘܪܐ ܡܫܬܓܪܒ ܠܐܠ ܩܕܡ ܡܐܬܝܬܗ
ܡܢ ܫܘܠܗܒܝܬܐ ܢܚܘܪ ܠܥܠܡܐ ܘܗܘ ܡܫܬܠܗܒܝܢ
ܡܫܕܪ ܩܠܐ ܘܙܥ ܡܠܐܟܐ ܠܐܪܒܥ ܦܢܝܬܐ
ܘܩܐܙܐ ܘܡܥܝܪ ܠܥܢܝܕܘܗܝ ܘܡܫܬܢܝܢ
ܪܓܙܐ ܡܢܐ ܘܡܣܘܚܕܗ ܠܚܠܐ ܢܦܠ
ܘܕܗ ܡܠܐܟܝܗܝ ܘܩܥܛܐ ܘܥܡܗ ܡܢ ܥܠܝܗܘܢ
ܐܠܦ ܐܠܦܝܢ ܩܝܡܐ ܚܝܠܬܐ ܘܪܒܘܬܐ
ܘܡܪܬܢܝܢ ܟܠ ܚܕ ܚܒܠܐ ܘܢܘܪܐ ܕܘܥܐ ܐܚܕ
ܡܥܢܝܢܐ ܐܙܠܐ ܘܐܙܥܝܢ ܥܠܗ ܡܢܗ ܡܢܗ
ܘܡܚܠܢܐ ܡܣܐ ܘܡܚܕ ܣܡܠܐ ܘܩܘܪܢܕܠܝܬܐ
ܡܢܗܝܢ ܡܚܙܐ ܘܒܝܥܬܗܝܢ ܚܬܐܐ ܐܝܟ ܡܚܩܬܐ
ܘܐܠܐ ܡܠܐ ܒܩܥܗܝܢ ܚܕܗܝܢ ܡܢ ܐܚܪܢܐ

A stormy sea of fire will precede His coming,
by its flame it will prove the worlds and so they will be consumed.
He will send the voice of his archangel to the four corners,

it will dissolve and destroy their compositions and their natures.
A horn will sound and at its blare the world will fall,
and those asleep in Sheol will stir from their sleep.
There will come with him crowds in glowing flame,
clouds of light will bear him with great fanfare.
The earth will pass away and cause all generations to mourn;
judgement will come and the day of retribution will draw near.
Graves will disappear and the dead will spew forth like springs,
and all come forth from perdition without corruption.

SUMMARY

Adam was the pinnacle and culmination of all beauty of creation (1–50)

The demise of Adam and the dissolution of his composition (51–109)

The purpose of every detail of Adam's constitution (110–149)

Adam and Eve adorned in garments of light; extinguished by the Evil One (150–191)

The Son came down to restore Adam's lost image (192–235)

The second coming, the new creation and the end of the old (236–277)

The new creation will be one of unending light (278–315)

The end of the world is death and dissolution (316–353)

An exhortation to forsake temporal things and look to the eternal (354–377)

Adam will rise up again at the general resurrection (378–417)

The spiritual nature of the new creation (418–437)

The same Adam will rise up and regain his garment of light (438–453)

Text and Translation

Jacob of Sarug

Mêmrâ 72: On the Creation of Adam and the Resurrection of the Dead[1]

I. Adam was the Pinnacle and Culmination of All Beauty of Creation

1   At the beginning, the creation of Adam was very great,[2]
but by his own will he brought himself down to a great fall.[3]
By his Creator, he was a god of flesh[4] to creation,
but by his free will he aligned himself with a beast and became like it.
5   The Good One who formed him placed and set him in the heights of Eden,[5]
but the evil one who hated him cast him down into the depths of a grave.

---

[1] Alwan prefers the title, "On the Constitution of Adam"; see the relevant discussion in the introduction, above, p. 17.

[2] Cf. Gen 1:26, Ps 8:5–9, et al.

[3] Isaac the Teacher's unedited "Homily on Adam and Eve" begins with an even longer lament over Adam losing his high station and falling into the depths; here it is put on the lips of Adam himself, summed up in the verse: "I who was richer than all have now fallen lower than all; Ms. Vat. Syr. 120, f. 155r; see E. Mathews, "Isaac of Antioch and the Literature of Adam and Eve."

[4] Jacob also calls Adam a "god of flesh" in his "Homily on the Sixth Day of Creation", Bedjan, III.109, and "like a God" in his "Homily on the First Day of Creation", line 123. Isaac the Teacher uses the same phrase in his "Homily on Adam and Eve", Ms. Vat. Syr. 120, f. 161r. Ephrem calls Adam a "second God over creation"; see *Commentary on Genesis* XXVI.1. In contrast, Narsai only calls Adam "kin to the angels"; see his "Homily on the Constitution of Adam and Eve", 7.

[5] Cf. Gen 2:15. Jacob here means this literally, following Ephrem who says that the base of the mountain of Paradise is higher than the summit of all the other mountains; see *Hymns on Paradise* I.4.

ܐܶܘܕ ܝܰܥܩܘܒ

ܡܐܡܪܐ. ܝܓ.

ܘܥܠ ܕܢܺܝܐܝܠ ܕܐܘܦ ܗܘ ܣܳܒܐ ܥܰܬܺܝܩܐ.

B 072

152

1
ܡܢ ܩܕܘܫܐ ܣܓܝ ܪܚܝܡ ܕܢܝܐܝܠ ܕܐܘܦ:
ܘܕܪܓܫܬܗ ܥܕ ܒܗ ܗܥܠܐ ܘܐܬܐܝܠܕ ܠܗ܀
ܡܢ ܚܙܘܬܗ ܐܠܗܐ ܚܕܬܐ ܗܘܐ ܠܟܠܢܫܐ:
ܘܒܣܒܪܬܗ ܒܗ ܒܥܠܡܐ ܩܐܘܦܕ ܠܗ܀

5
ܠܐ ܓܝܪ ܟܚܟܬܗ ܠܢܒܝܐ ܕܚܢ ܐܢܐܢ ܣܒܕܗ:
ܘܟܣܦܐ ܘܥܠܘܗܝ ܠܢܬܘܗܥܐ ܘܥܕܐ ܗܣܝܗ ܥܒܟܠܐ܀

He was the great image⁶ in whom the wisdom of the Exalted One was evident,
and in him was proclaimed that knowledge that cannot be attained.⁷
His form declared how wise was the One who formed him,
10 but his death proclaimed how shameful was his deceiver.
By this image the Lord manifested His wisdom,
but by it Satan also manifested his bitterness.
The Good One also wove a chamber of light for him in Eden,
but that evil counterpart built a house of darkness for him in Sheol.
15 Heaven and earth, the sea and the dry land, and all that is in them,⁸
hidden worlds, and the immense body of all creatures,
beauties of every sort of creature were set out onto their forms,
as well as every formation of the places and their layouts.
He created all things beautiful when He created them according to their natures,⁹
20 and He came and brought all their beauty to a culmination in the image of Adam.¹⁰
He enclosed in that image all the colors that are in natures,
so that one might see in it all worlds and all places.
To see it is a small matter, but to examine it is a very great thing,
for bound up in it are all creatures and their formation.
25 Although no one is capable of seeing the end of [all] places,
in Adam one can see the height and depth, breadth and length.

---

⁶ Cf. Gen 1:26, et al.

⁷ This phrase was an apparently popular one in early Syriac literature; cf. Ephrem, *Letter to Publius*, 30, and Isaac of Antioch, *Homily* VII.xxx. Jacob himself also uses the phrase elsewhere; see his "Homily on the Sixth Day of Creation", Bedjan, III. 108, and "Was Adam Created Mortal or Immortal", Alwan II.150.

⁸ Cf. Ps 145(146):6.

⁹ Cf. Gen 1:31.

¹⁰ Compare Jacob's "Homily on the verse, *Come, let us make man in our own image after our likeness*," where all the beauty of creation is revealed in Christ, the image of God; Alwan I.242. For the importance of the concept of Adam as 'Image of God' for Jacob, see Bou Mansour, *La Théologie de Jacques de Saroug*, I.68–134.

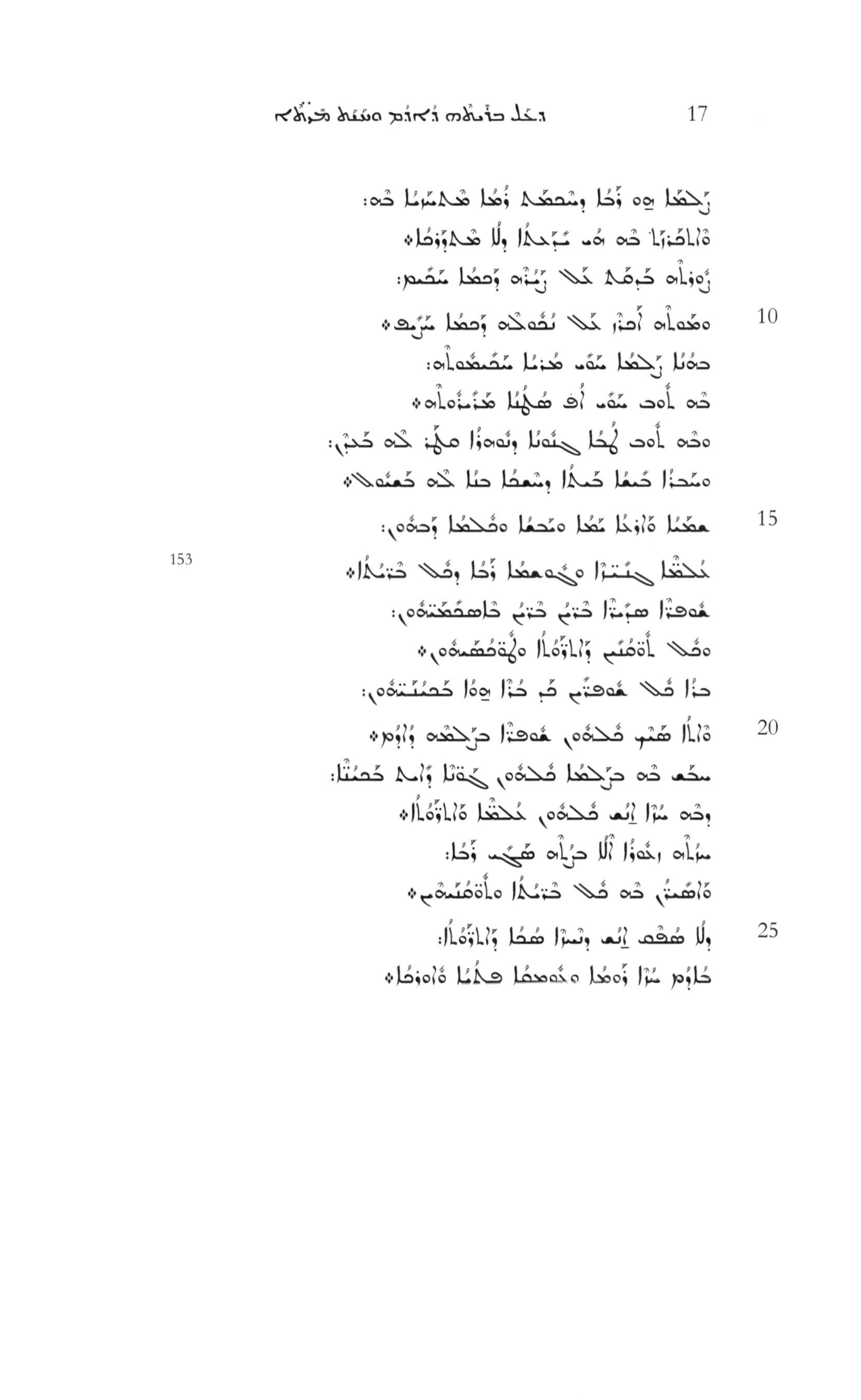

All natures, both those endowed with senses and those that are not,
the Wise One of the ages set in [Adam]'s creation when He created him.
The Creator mixed fire and air with dust and water,[11]
and He painted[12] him as an image to manifest His wisdom to the world.
And into these He blew a living fire[13] and in marvelous fashion
established man and gave him senses for [his] activity.
All beauties of all creatures were culminated in him,
so that in him one might see the nearness and the remoteness that belongs to natures.
Between the height and the depth He set him as an intermediary,
and He bound all sides in his person when He created him.
He made him to turn in six directions when He formed him;
height and depth and the four directions were bound to him.[14]
His Creator mixed [him] from opposing elements,
and set within him the power to subdue the wild animals.[15]
Fire and water went equally into the body of Adam,
so that in him it might be revealed how powerful was the wisdom of the Exalted One.
He joined clay and water with each other, and made them equal,
so that with one power they might hasten along with their companions.
Who is able to join with a yoke dust and water
and fire and air, and to infuse them into one body?
Who is capable of making heavy and light equal,

---

[11] Elsewhere Jacob also asserts that Adam was created from the four elements, see his "Homily on the Sixth Day of Creation", Bedjan III.113.

[12] The notion of God "painting" His image and other elements of creation was a common one among early Syriac poets, especially for Ephrem from whom Jacob no doubt inherited it.

[13] Cf. Gen 2:7.

[14] These six directions were created in the first six days; see Jacob's "Homily on the Sixth Day of Creation", Bedjan, III.102–103. In general, for much of what follows and for possible sources and parallels, see B. Sony, "L'anthropologie de Jacques de Saroug."

[15] Cf. Gen 2:19–20.

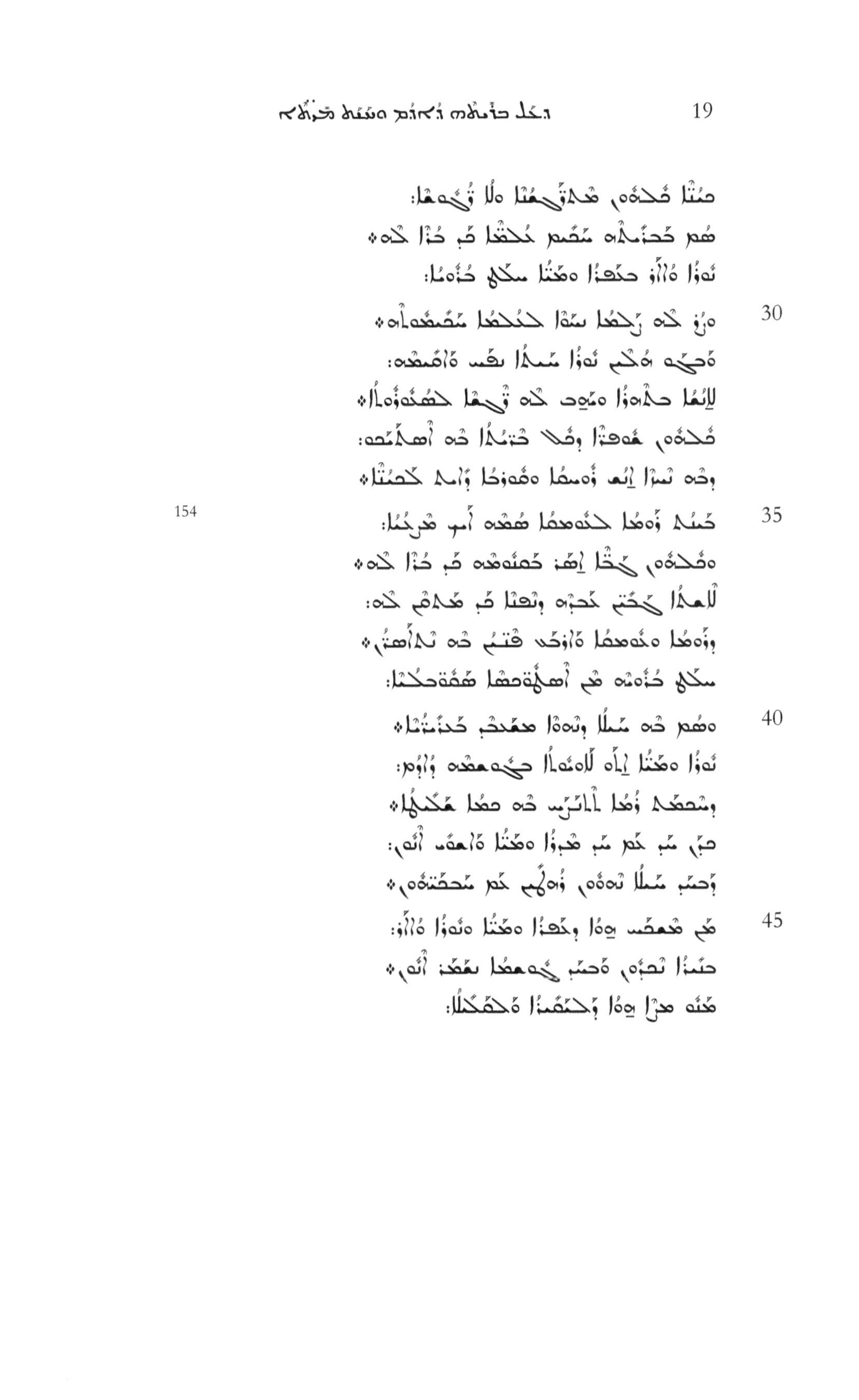

or of making their attributes coincide without any confusion?
Who has the ability to unite cold and hot,
50   and to harness them within a single body?

II. THE DEMISE OF ADAM AND THE DISSOLUTION OF HIS COMPOSITION

Who has ever painted for himself such an image,
and filled it with wonder for it to be a marvel in the world?
The image is glorious and it proclaims marvelous things about its Creator:
How wise, how omnipotent, and how powerful He is![16]
55   Wisdom painted a great image full of wonder,
brought it in and set it between the worlds so that they could gaze upon it.
She[17] loaded it up with adornments that all creatures might be seen in it,
but it forgot its nature and handed itself over to death that it may see its own fall.
Beauty fell down to the dust and became an object of shame;
60   because it transgressed the command of its Lord, it was handed over to death.[18]
All creation is a great city which the Just One built,[19]

---

[16] Jacob addresses God directly with a similar ejaculation; see his "Homily on the Sixth Day of Creation", Bedjan, III.105.

[17] I.e., Wisdom.

[18] Cf. Gen 3:3. This line has been added from the text published by Alwan; it is inserted here as it is clearly required by the line parallelism.

[19] Jacob refers to creation both as a city (see his "Homily on the Sixth Day of Creation", Bedjan, III.108) and as a house (see his "Homily on the Sixth Day of Creation", Bedjan, III.104–106); Narsai uses both in apposition in his "Homily on the Constitution of Adam and Eve", 3: "In the world, the royal city." Whatever the appellation, the idea that God created everything and then introduced the newly created Adam is an ancient one. Generally associated with Gregory of Nyssa, see his *On the Making of Man*, it also has Jewish roots, see L. Ginzberg, *The Legends of the Jews*, I.49.

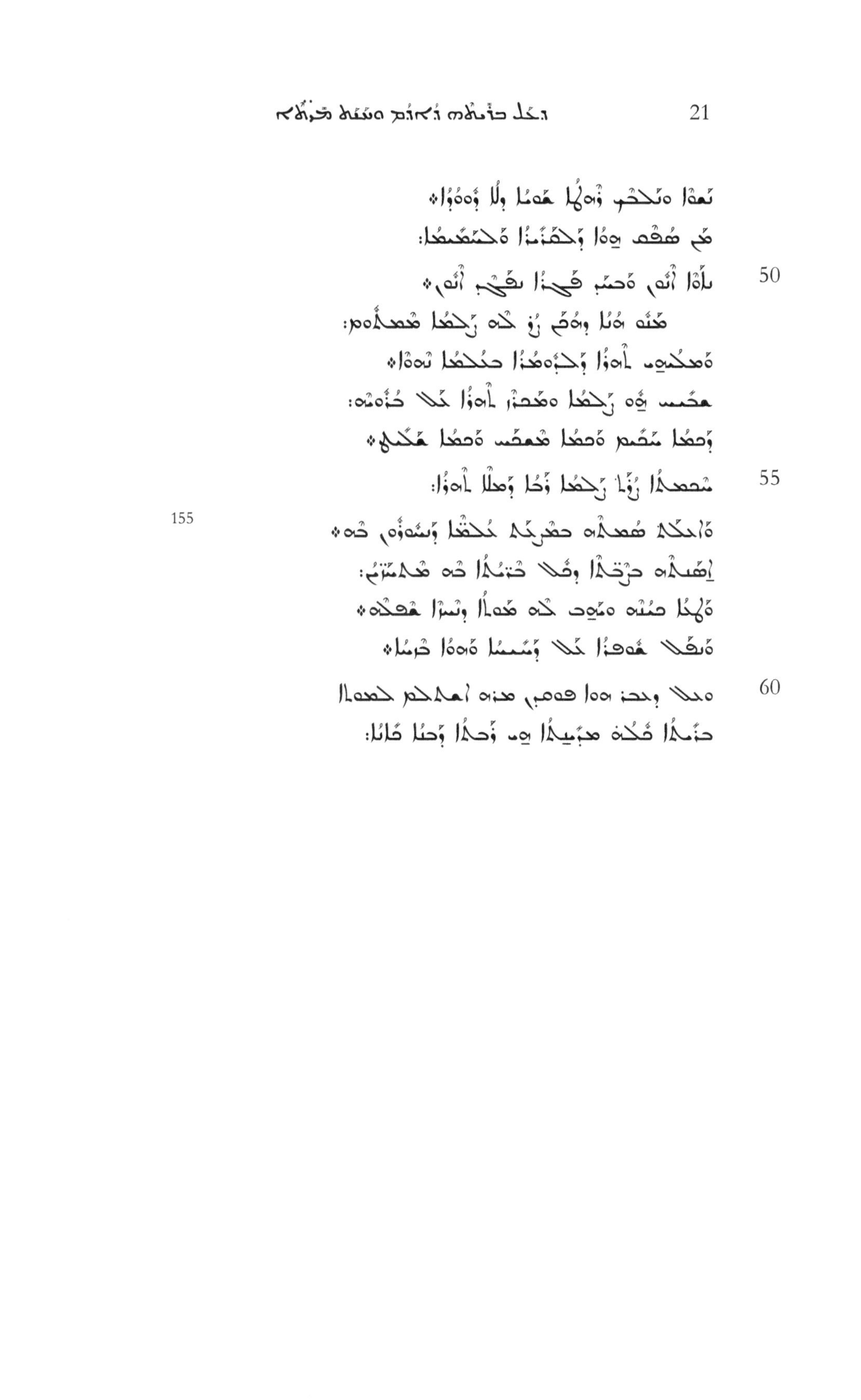

He established for Himself therein a rational icon and made him its lord.[20]
He painted an image for Himself and set it in the great city that He built,
but the evil one was envious of the beauty of the image of the Great King.

65 He sent a serpent and it bit that image by the deceit that it wrought,[21]
from that bile its adornments fell off into the dust of the earth.
Sin ensnared it and handed it over to death in order to plunder it,
it broke it, cast it down, perverted it, trampled on it and it became dust.
At the demise [of that image] those elements that had been bound were dissolved,
70 and with them those rational senses that had been bound were destroyed.
The four equal things fell apart and each was separated from its companion,
and destroyed the five along with them, and their composition came to an end.
The body was yoked to the four and it ran along like a chariot,
and the five senses stood upon it like charioteers.
75 Then death came and unhitched the yokes and the guides,
and every course of that great image fell and it came to its end.
It separated the cold from the hot and put an end to their operations,
as well as the moist from the dry and their functions came to an end.
And as soon as it cut off these two, one from the other,
80 the five perished and the nine came to an end as if they had never been.
Sight, hearing, taste, touch, and smell all perished,
for these five had moved together equally with the four.
Along with the elements that it loosed from [their] ways,

---

[20] See also his "Homily on the Sixth Day of Creation", Bedjan III.108–109.

[21] Cf. Gen 3:1–7.

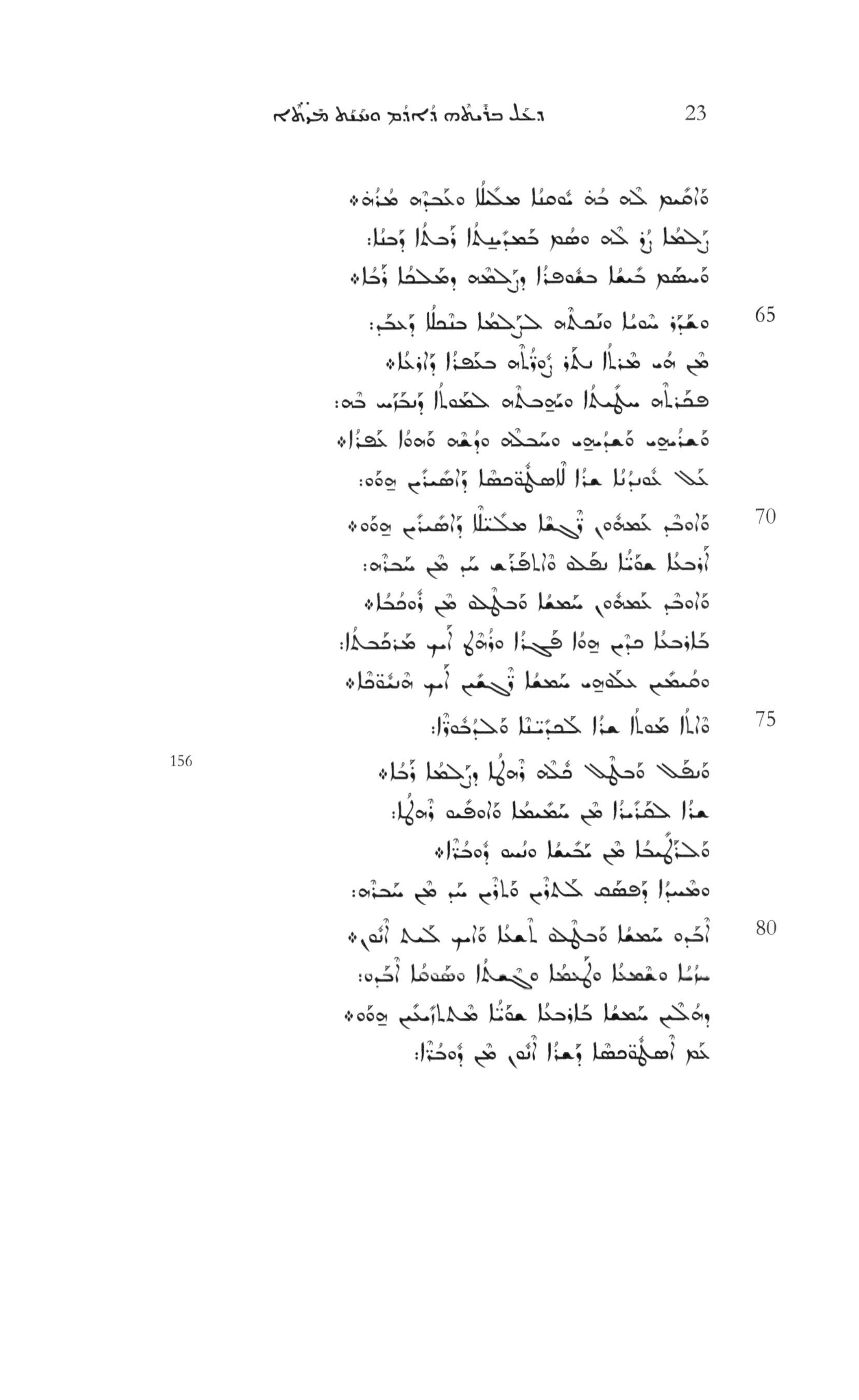

those senses also ceased, no longer to move according to their functions.
85 For no longer would it see, hear, or touch,
nor would it taste or smell, for each had been dispersed.
For death scattered it and put it into the corners of a grave,
and all the beauties that had been assembled were destroyed by it.
Out of the elements it had been constituted and stood like a pillar,
90 by that hidden power that had given it its nature from nothing.
Because it had eaten from the tree and despised the commandment,
it caused its own dissolution in death and its activity came to an end.
And the elements that He had gathered up, it scattered,
and the senses that He had ordered, it destroyed, trampled and brought to an end.
95 And those comely, desirable beauties came to an end and were destroyed,
and all the beautiful adornments fell into destruction.
It had no speech, no sound, not even a whisper
for death had closed its mouth in silence and its speech ceased.
It fell from the height and was thrust down as a companion of death,
100 in its nakedness it went down to Sheol like a feeble one.
On the thread of the soul like a necklace of pearls,
it had been entirely strung and arrayed with pleasing limbs;
all the various types of beauty were intermingled in it,
and it had become one great beauty with no bounds.
105 The dragon came, stung the thread of life and it fell off,
and behold that lovely necklace burst and rolled into the bowels of Sheol.
Precious gems and costly pearls
had been embroidered on it and it had been a great crown of light.
The viper hissed and in its rebellion cast away the crown;

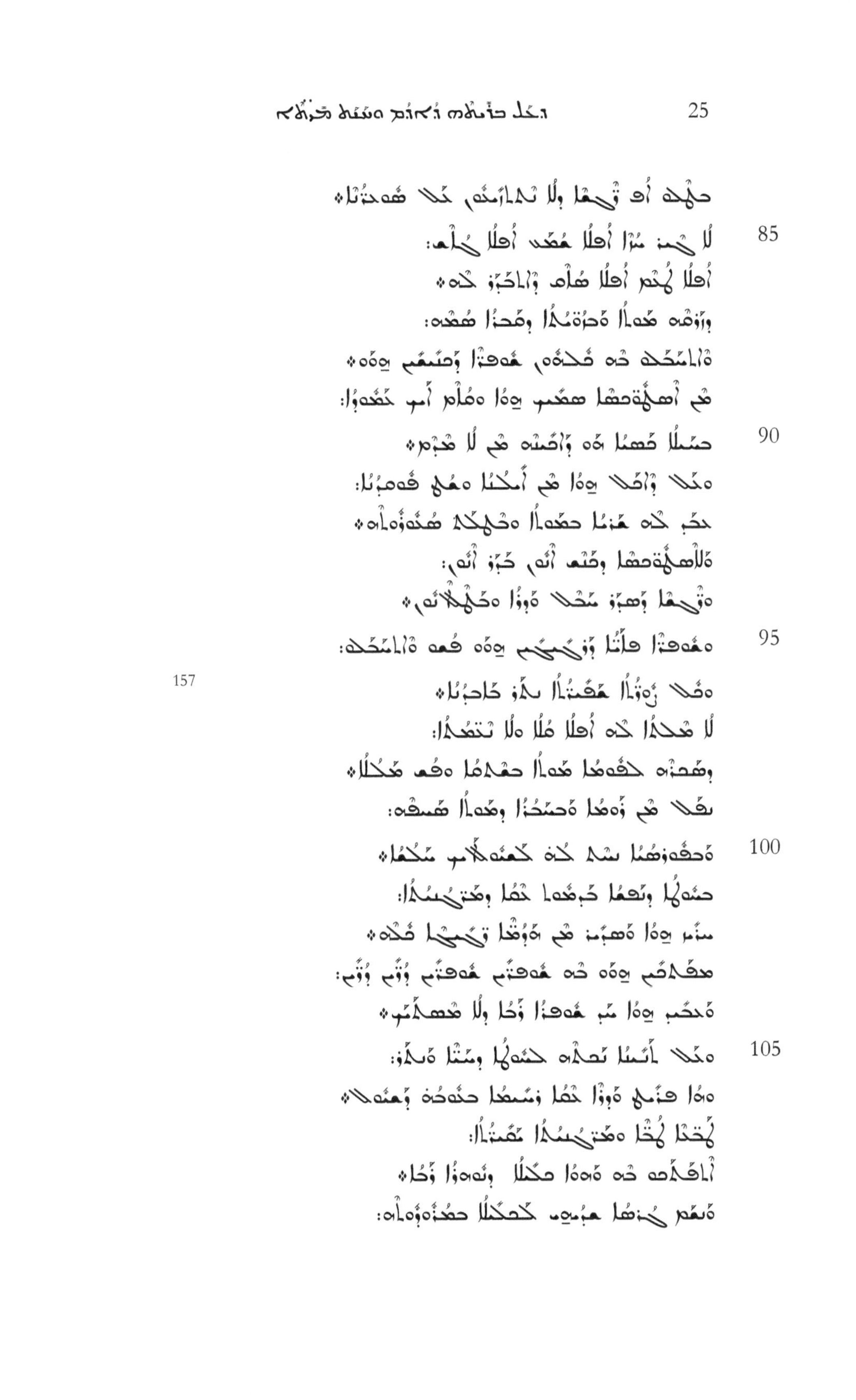

III. THE PURPOSE OF EVERY DETAIL OF ADAM'S CONSTITUTION

110   its gems were scattered and its beauty dispersed into the grave.

       In his great beauty Adam was even more glorious than a crown,
and among creatures there was no other beauty comparable to his.
His Jeweler set springs of light atop his crown,[22]
so as if from on high he might gaze upon the creatures that surrounded him.

115   Beneath him He fashioned feet for racing like a chariot,
so that with them he might travel wherever he wished to go.
On his flanks He fashioned hands and on them ten fingers,
that with them he might lay hold of the sea, the dry land and the whole world.
He fashioned a brain to be a home for his mind,

120   so that it might reside in a lofty dwelling like a god.
He made for him a palate that he might be able to discriminate tastes,
and He set taste therein that he might distinguish sweet from bitter.
He opened nostrils for him so that they might be a path for odors
by which he might discern a putrid smell from a sweet one.

125   He bore out a passage for hearing and surrounded it with the form of a seashell,
that sounds might circulate and enter in gently through it.
In his breast is the heart wherein all his thoughts are gathered,
so that as if from a great storehouse it may put forth all its treasures.
Speech is through his mouth and with his lips the distinction of sounds,

---

[22] For all the following components of the creation of Adam, compare the similar description in Jacob's "Homily on the Sixth Day of Creation", Bedjan, III.113–115.

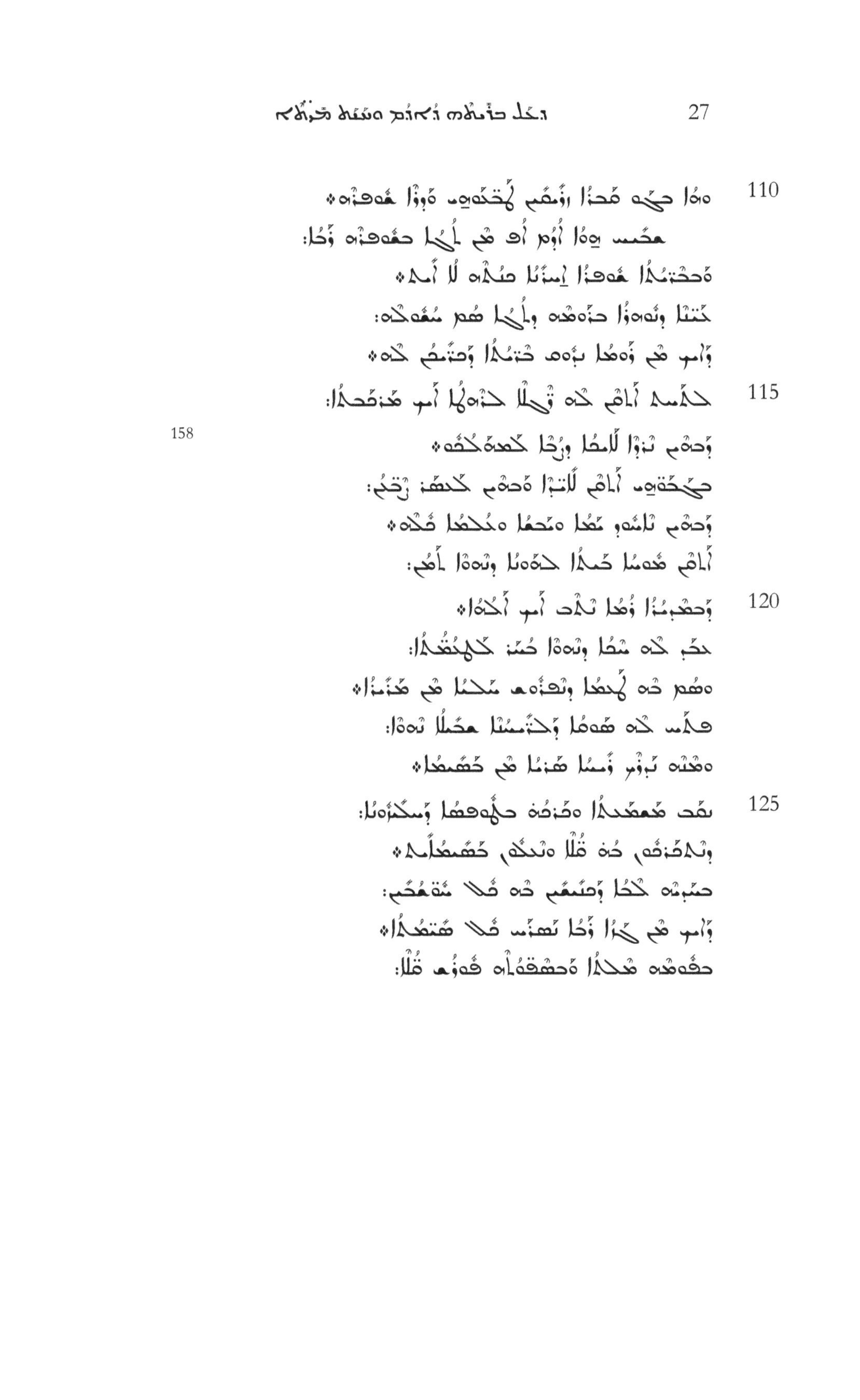

130 eyebrows for expressions, and He adorned the pupils with eyelashes.
In one member He placed bitterness and anger like a fire,
by which he might be inflamed against wickedness whenever it occurred.
In another He placed them to be the receptacle for sadness,
that he might feel remorse for evils when they were committed.
135 To yet another He granted that it should serve for cheerfulness,
so that when good is done his countenance might be glad and joyful.
Various things for each limb did the Wise One of the ages
form and arrange on that beautiful image when He fashioned it.
Out of nothing the Creator made a very great thing,
140 that by its own wisdom it might be lord of everything.
But the serpent came and spewed its bile upon that beautiful thing,
and turned it into putrid and fetid filth in the darkness.
This comeliness fell into the pit that it might be tormented therein,
and every quality of its beauty was trampled and destroyed in it.
145 Because he had been exalted he was brought low and became a mockery;
he fell from his station, embraced his clay and took hold of his lowliness.
His station had been high! Would that he had held fast to his high station!
But he did not remain [there]; his chasm was deep and full of terrors.
His creation was great, exalted, comely and full of beauties,

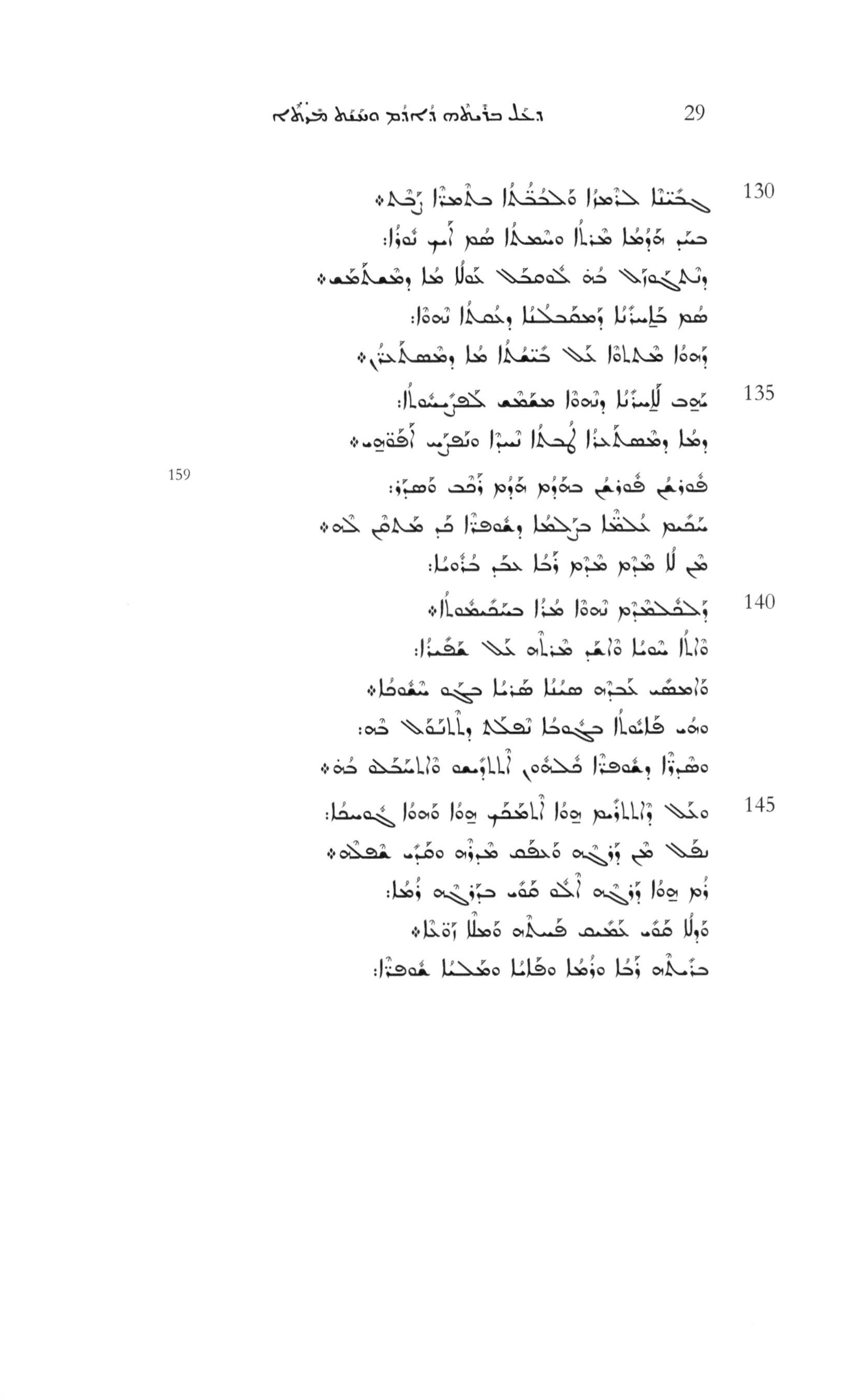

159

IV. Adam and Eve adorned in garments of light; extinguished by the Evil One

      The hidden signal[23] of the Maker had gathered up some clay,
took it and formed mud, then He mixed it and united it with air.[24]
He tempered it with fire and gave it a life-giving spirit,[25]
and it became an image that is dry and moist, hot and cold.
150 He mixed in the elements as if they were colors and blended them in,
and He made from them a comely form full of beauty.
From choice pigments that He had selected He painted for Himself an image,
and made it a bridegroom in this great bridal chamber that He had framed.
He adorned Eve as a virgin bride and gave her to Adam,
160 and into her dowry He put the sea, the dry land, and the air.[26]
All the worlds gathered for the great marriage feast that He had prepared,
the bridal couple were radiant in their crowns and their raiment.
He covered them in magnificent light and in elegant radiance,
and He left them among the trees to enjoy their delights.[27]

---

[23] Syr., *remzô*, indicating God's incorporeal motionless 'nod' is a key concept for Jacob; see Alwan, "Le 'remzo' selon la pensée de Jacques de Saroug". In his "Homily on the Sixth Day of Creation", Bedjan, III.109, Jacob distinguishes the creation of all things by God's *remzô* and His creation of Adam by His hands.

[24] Gen 2:7.

[25] Cf. 1 Cor 15:45.

[26] Another description of the creation of Eve is found in Jacob's "Homily on the Sixth Day of Creation", Bedjan, III.104, 124.

[27] Cf. Gen 2:9–10.

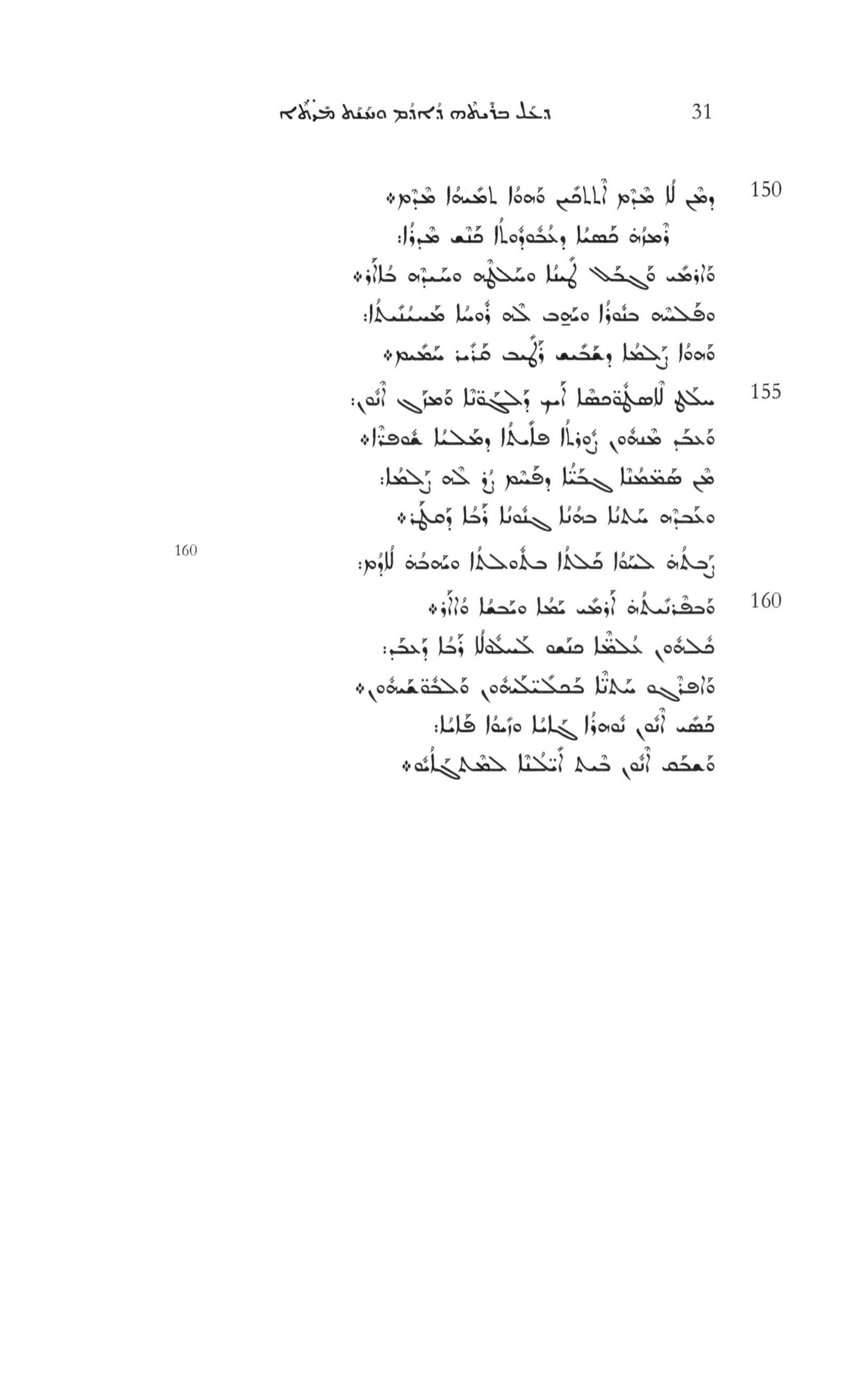

165 He gave them every tree and their fruits as a wedding present,
and the garden exulted in the bride and bridegroom for they were beloved.
The tree of life was in the great bridal chamber of Eden;
it was concealed, to be for that luminous couple when they were perfected.[28]
But that tree of knowledge which was full of death,
170 stood out in the open beside it like something beautiful.
And so that they would know who was the Lord who had exalted them,
He set down a law that they should not eat from that tree.
The entire garden He gave to these new children He had established,
only one single tree did He give in order to test them.[29]
175 The malicious one entered and cast divisions into that wedding feast,
he stole away the bride, whispered, lied, beguiled and deceived her.
A[s a] hawk among innocent and glorious doves he entered and stood,
and made them fly off from that great nest of Eden.
Envy came upon those beautiful ones and it troubled them,
180 the deceit of the serpent infatuated, corrupted and tripped them up.
They went ahead rashly and ate from the tree that was full of death,[30]
disgrace and dishonor sprang immediately upon them.
Their adornments and their crowns were reduced to naught,

---

[28] Jacob follows Ephrem here in having the tree of life concealed from Adam and Eve "so that the tree would not cause any great struggle for them by its beauty and thus double their agony"; see his *Commentary on Genesis*, II.17.

[29] Cf. Gen 2:16–17. Jacob reiterates this in his homily "*Was Adam created mortal or immortal?*", Alwan III.131. Ephrem too highlights the fact that God gave to Adam and Eve all of Paradise, with the exception of one single tree, and then almost only for the pretense of a trial; see his *Commentary on Genesis* II.17. See also discussion in L. Van Rompay, "Humanity's Sin in Paradise."

[30] Cf. Gen 3:6.

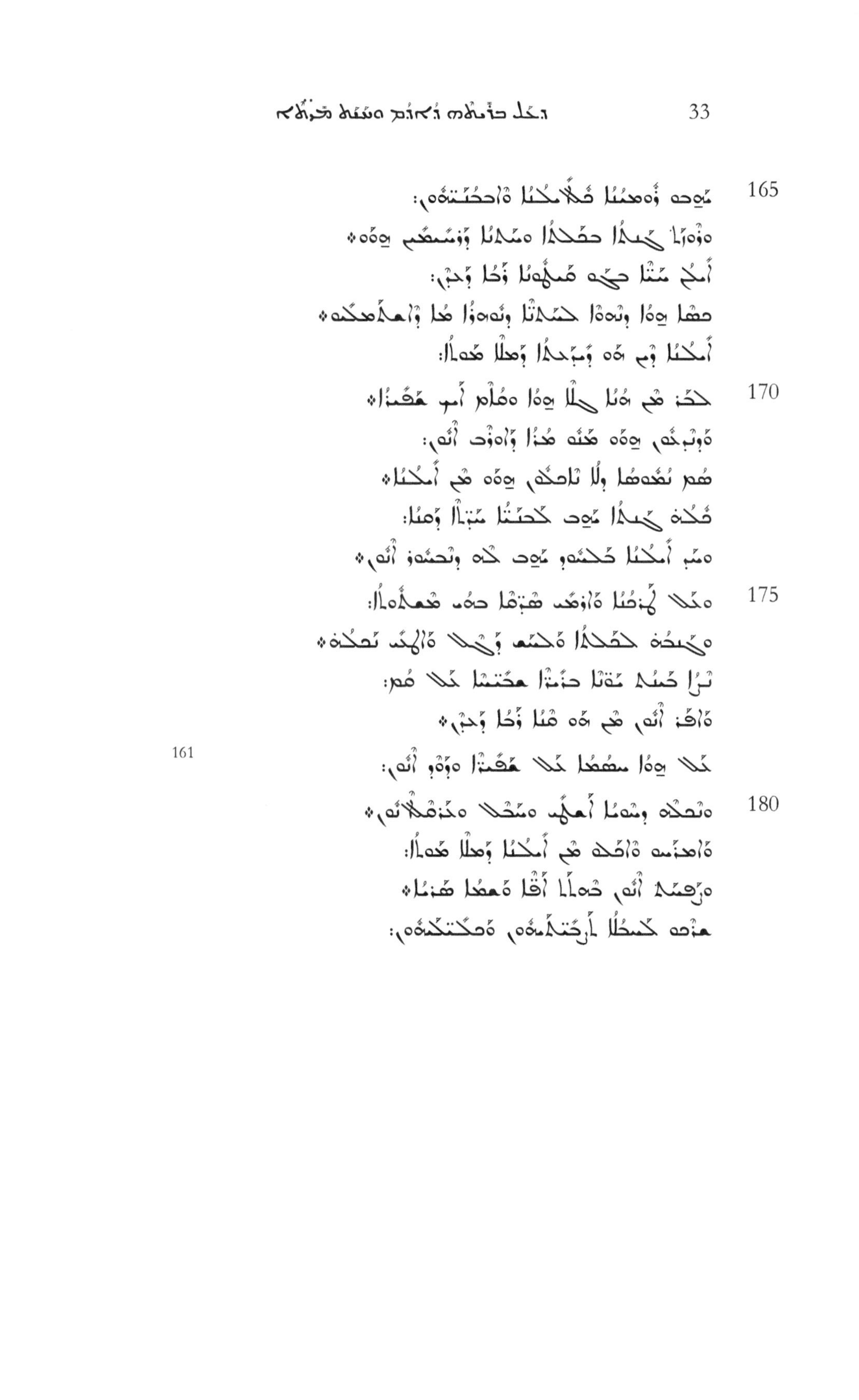

their beauty was extinguished and their joyful sounds came to an end.
185 The serpent snatched away the garment of light[31] in which they were clothed,
and in great terror, those thieves stood there naked.[32]
The fruit of desire stripped them and brought shame upon them,
it destroyed and ruined all the beauty in which they had been arrayed.
The image that the Divinity had painted went down to destruction,
190 then death trampled it down and thrust it into Sheol.
Honor passed away from the honored one and disgrace enveloped him,
that great one fell from his greatness and took hold of lowliness.

V. THE SON CAME DOWN TO RESTORE ADAM'S LOST IMAGE

Because of the great fall of this great image,
the Son of the King went down to restore His image that had become corrupted.[33]
195 Our Lord conducted a great search on behalf of the lost sheep,
he carried it on his shoulder to make them exactly one hundred.[34]
The Most High descended into the most extreme lowliness,
to raise back to the heights that high one who had fallen into that depth.
For his sake He came at the end to raise him back up,

---

[31] See Jacob's "Homily on the Sixth Day of Creation", Bedjan, III.125; similar wording in Jacob's "Homily on the Expulsion of Adam from Paradise", Alwan, III.573, 640, 646. Early Syriac writers often used this image of garment of light for pre-fallen and redeemed mankind; see S.P. Brock, *The Luminous Eye*, 85–97, idem., "Clothing Metaphors as a means for Theological Expression," and, specifically for Jacob's use of this image, T. Kollamparampil *Salvation in Christ according to Jacob of Serugh*, 179–180, 220–222.

[32] Cf. Gen 3:7.

[33] This restoration, or recovery, of the lost Adam fulfilled the single lacking in Christ according to Jacob; see his "Homily on Epiphany," 201–212.

[34] Cf. Matt 18:12, Luke 15:4.

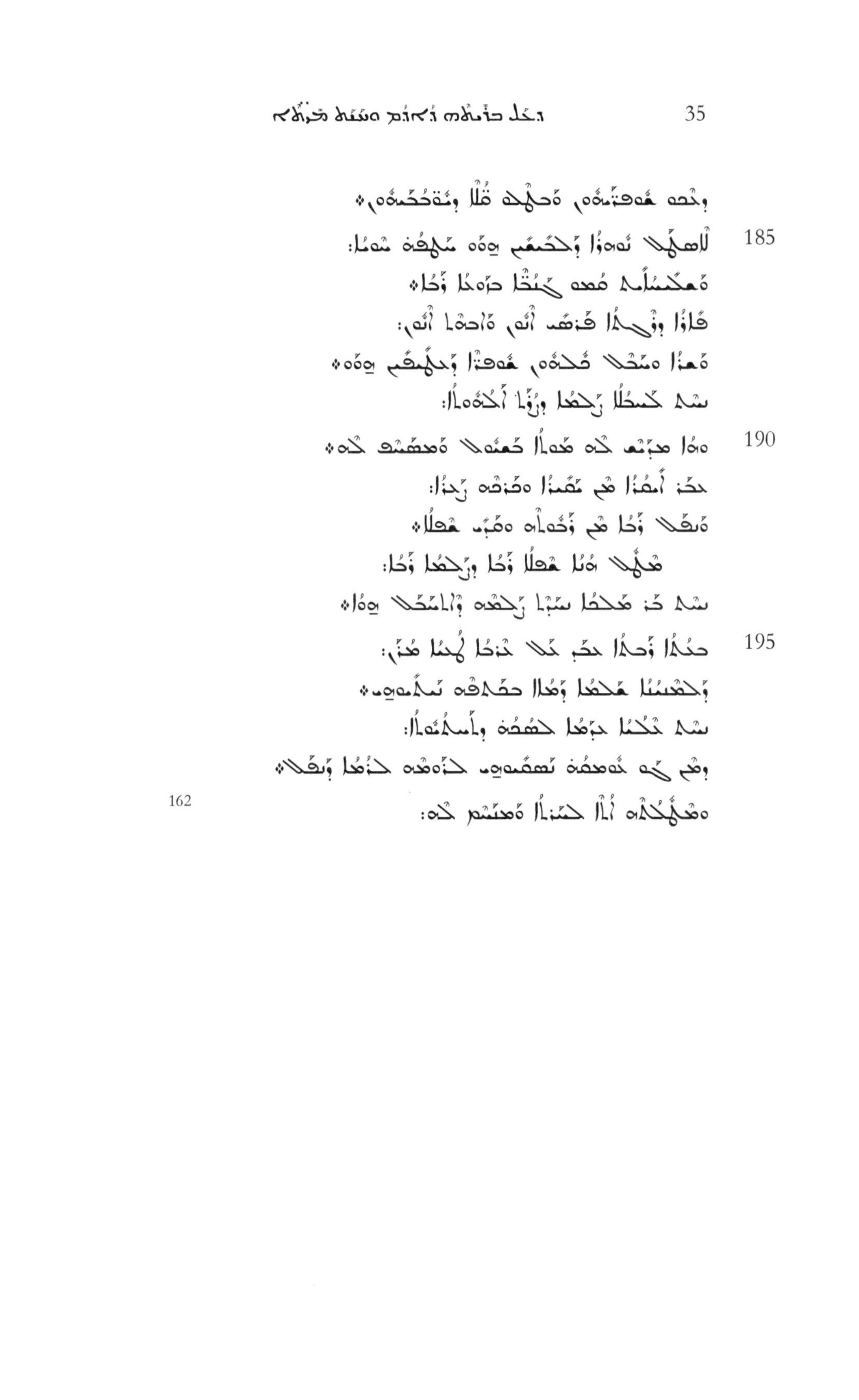

200   and to return him to that first place which had been promised to him.
In mercy He formed him, in mercy He delivered him from robbers,
and in mercy He will come again at the end and raise him back up.[35]
With a single thought that was neither a new one nor a change of mind,
mercy dawned on three occasions and so was completed:
205   The first time, He painted him in His image out of dust,[36]
the second time, He redeemed him through the blood of His Only-Begotten.[37]
then the last time, He will call out with a voice and raise him up,[38]
thus, in a three-fold way, He finishes him, makes him whole, and perfects him.
He will shake off the dust from his face and renew him,
210   He will raise him up without corruption into the spiritual light.
He formed him, redeemed him, and will raise him up; in him He mixes Himself,
so that he might be with Him, in Him, like Him, and for Him.
When He created him He brought him into a contest of righteousness,
and when He redeemed him He gave him freedom from his captors.
215   When He raises him up He will bequeath him the good things He had promised,
so that Adam might possess everything of His without distinction.
When did Adam repay his Lord for these great rewards?
Or when will he ever be able to repay Him for His beautiful things?

---

[35] For the importance for Jacob of God's mercy in creation and redemption, see his "Homily on Epiphany," 215–216, "Homilies on the Nativity," I.103–120, III.85–90, and discussions in T. Bou Mansour, *La Théologie de Jacques de Saroug*, I.28–33, and T. Kollamparampil, *Salvation in Christ according to Jacob of Serugh*, 220–229.

[36] Cf. Gen 1:26.

[37] Cf. Eph 1:7, 1 Pet 1:18–19.

[38] 1 Thess 4:16.

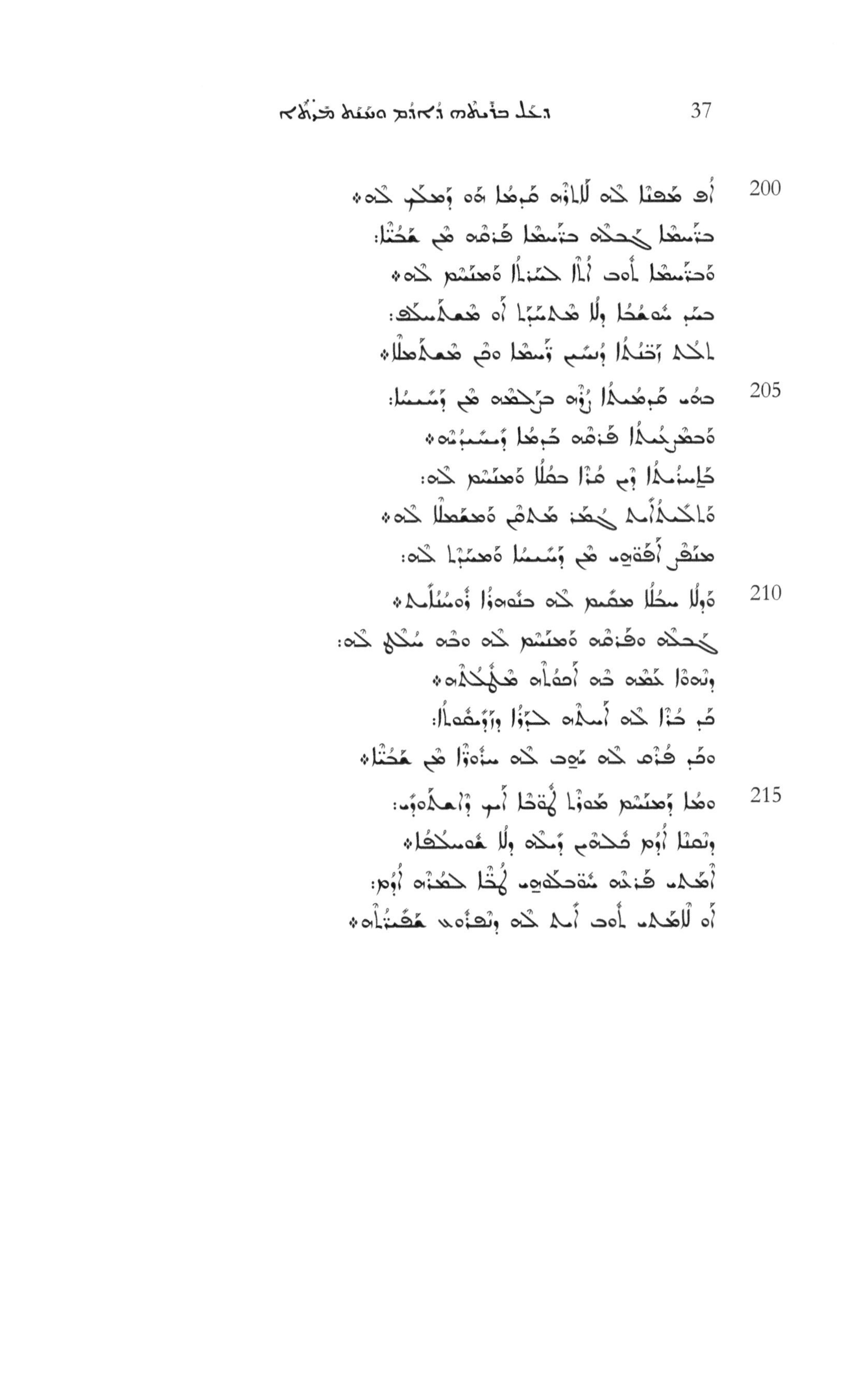

What did he repay Him when He gave him his nature from nothing,
220   or what did he give Him who crucified His Son on his behalf?
What will he repay when He raises him up from the dust?
All these things were free on account of [His] incomprehensible mercy.
Adam has three good things from God:
two have already come and one will come at the end of time.
225   Let not that one who is sure that the two have come to pass
be in any doubt about the one that is to come; it has its time like its companions.
It is a good and great thing that Adam came to be from nothing,
and likewise that he was redeemed by the blood of the Son of God.[39]
That he will be raised up from the dust is also a good thing,
230   there is one single power that accomplishes these three things.
If He had not created him He certainly would not have redeemed Him,
but because He did create and redeem him, mercy required that He also raise him up.
He will come at the end to accomplish everything in spiritual fashion,
and He will raise up His image from its fall so that it will never fall again.
235   He will come to complete the course of time and of cycles,
and when they are completed, He will put an end to the course of the great circuit.

VI. THE SECOND COMING, THE NEW CREATION AND THE END OF THE OLD

He will arise and come, and all ages will tremble at His coming,
His sign will rise up and all generations will quake before it.

---

[39] Cf. Eph 1:7, 1 Pet 1:18–19.

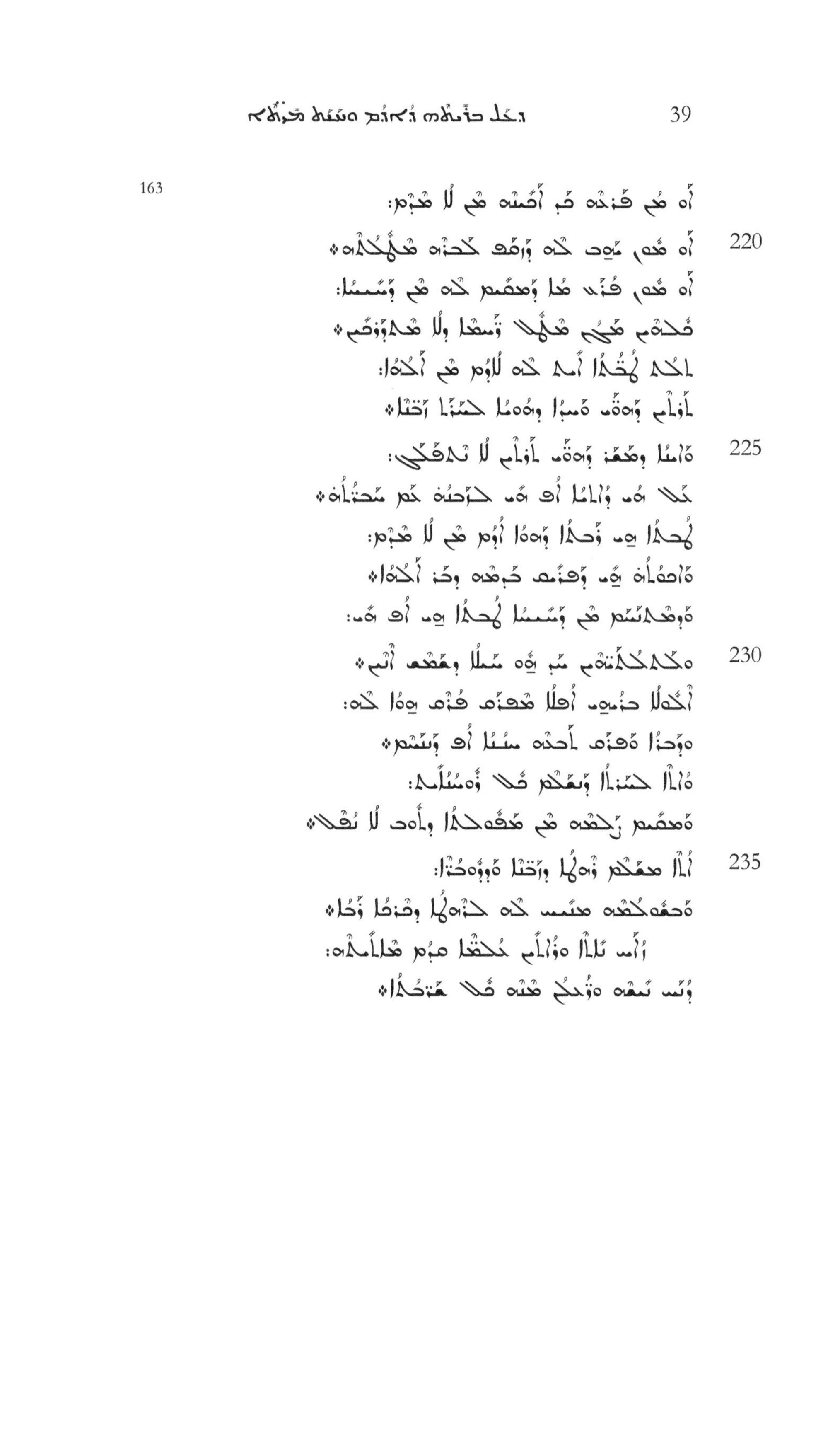

163

He will set out on His journey and the watchers will fly before His coming,
240 He will signal to thousands and His hosts will hasten before Him.
Legions and myriads will quake and He will cause them to tremble,
Ranks will fly alongside Him as well as orders of flame.
The ends [of the world] will quake at his swift legions,
for they will rain down burning coals and hurl down lightning and a great light.
245 In wonder He will go forth to effect judgement and righteousness,
and all ages will openly behold His great zeal.
The good ones will fly up to meet the King who stirred from His place,
and they will receive Him to be with Him as He had promised.
The company of Simon will meet the company of the House of Gabriel,
250 and His elect will come with Him, as will His angels.
The thousands of Paul with the ten thousands of the House of Michael[40]
will resound with Glorys and Hosannahs on their trumpets.
The Apostles of light along with those honored with thrones,
will come in great trembling along with the Judge in glory.
255 Creation will thunder along with the hosts before the Son of the King,
who will come with uprightness to judge the living and the dead.[41]
His voice will unhinge the composition of all creatures,
for in spiritual fashion He will refashion the world with no composition.
His signal will unhinge those elements that had been yoked,

---

[40] The phrase "House of Michael" is also found in Jacob's Homily on "*Was Adam created mortal or immortal?*", Alwan II.179; the intent here is clearly Simon and Paul as representative of the human race, and Gabriel and Michael of the angelic race.

[41] Cf. 2 Tim 4:1, 1 Pet 4:5.

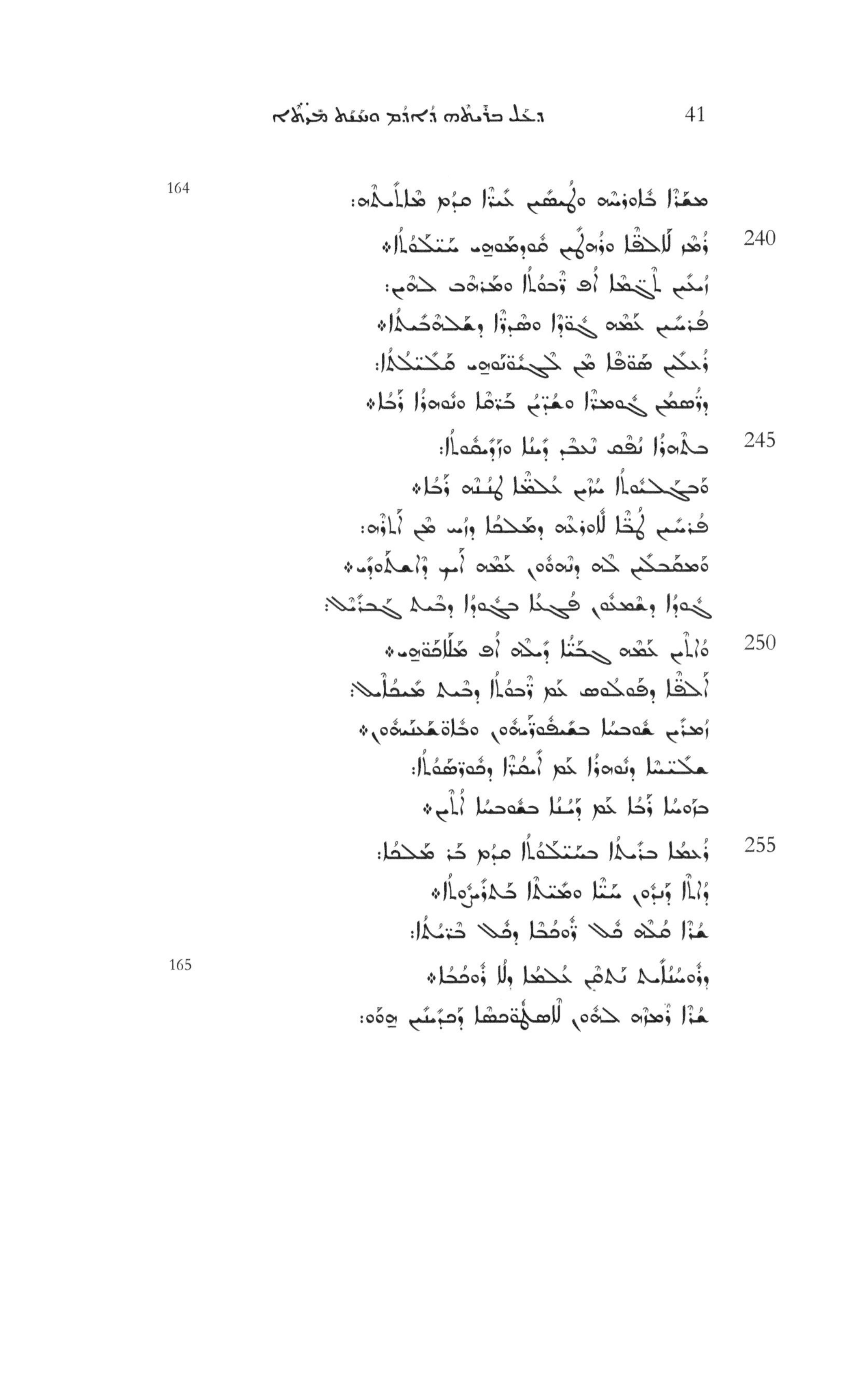

164

165

260	their temporal courses along with their movements will all come to an end.
	The sun will darken and the moon will pass away[42] along with their dwelling places,
	and the path of the hosts will come to an end for it will continue no longer.
	The order both of the four corners and their designations will come to an end,
	for they will no longer progress in their natures or by their functions.
265	The east will pass away with its lights and its rays,
	dawn will no longer rise there for there will be one dawn.
	When the sun darkens[43] and no longer travels on its course,
	even that quadrant in which it rose will be blotted out.
	The west will come to an end as will its name along with it,
270	for the lights will no longer set there at their [appointed] times.
	When they no longer exist, how will these hosts set?
	With no setting there will be no more west for it will be blotted out.
	As for the south quadrant through which all the lights had been coming,
	but when they are no longer there to come, its role too will have come to an end.
275	The north with its mountains was made a shelter in which they hid themselves,
	when they come to an end it will not be required for it will also have come to an end.
	The corners will have come to an end because their functions will have come to an end,
	for that system will no longer be suitable in the new world.

VII. THE NEW CREATION WILL BE ONE OF UNENDING LIGHT

Christ is the sun of that kingdom when it will be revealed

---

[42] Cf. Isa 60:19, Apoc 21:23.
[43] Cf. Matt 24:29, Mark 13:24.

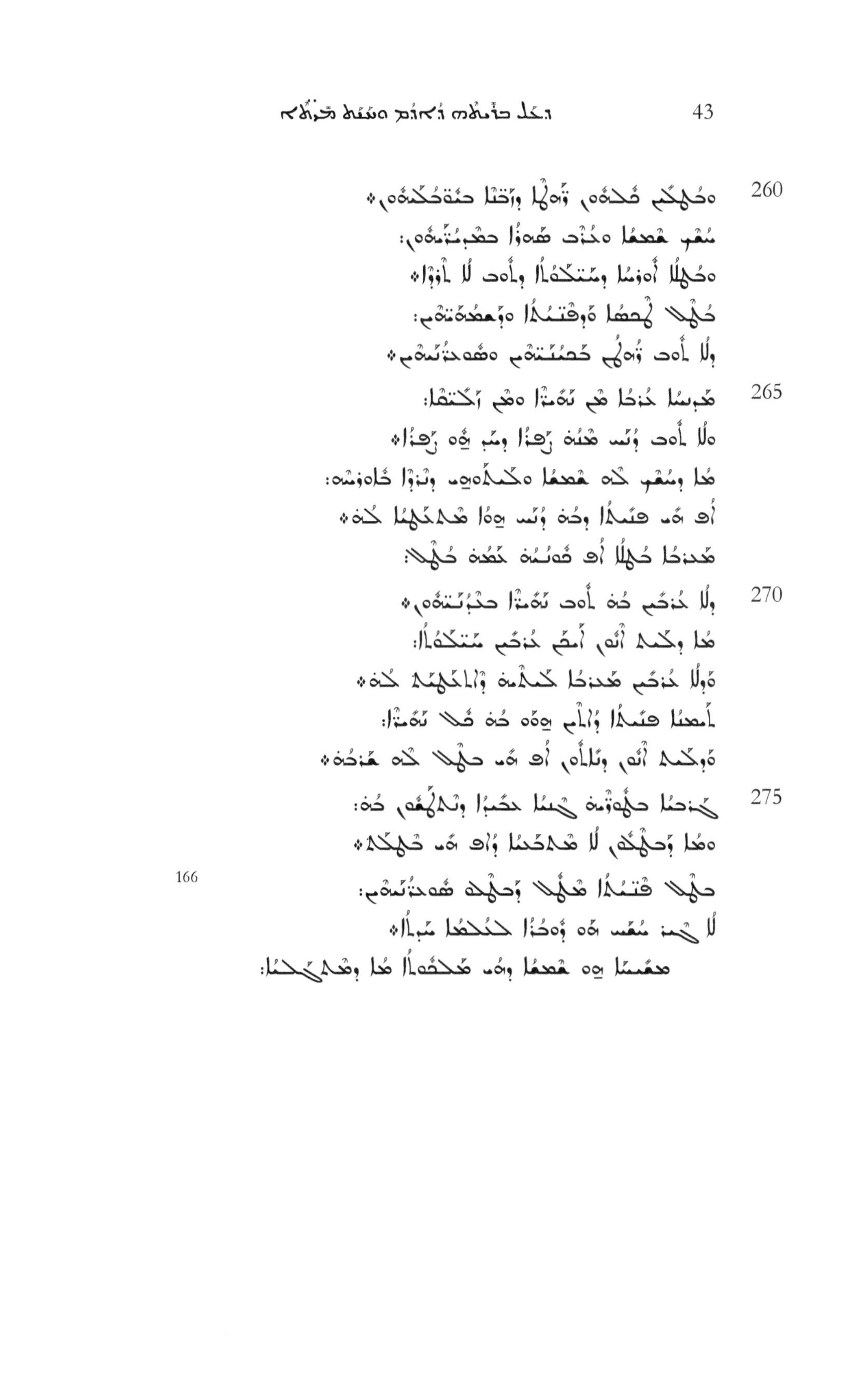

280 and He is the light that dawns and eclipses all [other] lights.[44]
The cycle of time will be broken and its course will come to an end,
it will stand in wonder and not go about on its courses.
Morning and evening will come to an end and not go around,
for one day will last forever – without change.[45]
285 There, nights and their courses will come to an end,
for the night that remains is one and it will stand still off to the left.
There will be neither a dawn nor an end to that night,
nor will there be an evening or any change on that day.
The darkness is cut off and stands off to the left side,
290 the light will dawn, rise and show itself on the right side.
The axis is broken and time will no longer pass there,
the bridge is cut down and the hosts will not pass over it.
Jesus is Lord there, the Sun of Righteousness,[46]
whom no evening with its darkness can obscure or change.
295 The Lord is one and the day of the great light is one–
an eternal light that is not subject to any darkness.
There is no more requirement for the sun to dawn or for the sun to set,
for Christ the dawn is not susceptible to change.
There the light is not subservient to the weaker elements,
300 that it should move in measured intervals from here to there.
By all and through all, with all and in all Christ dawns,
He is not contained in a sphere like the sun nor does He travel on its path.
He makes time pass by, but He does not ever pass with the times,
He changes moments with a signal but He is never changed.

---

[44] Cf. Apoc 21:23, 22:5.
[45] Cf. Zech 14:7.
[46] Cf. Mal 4:2.

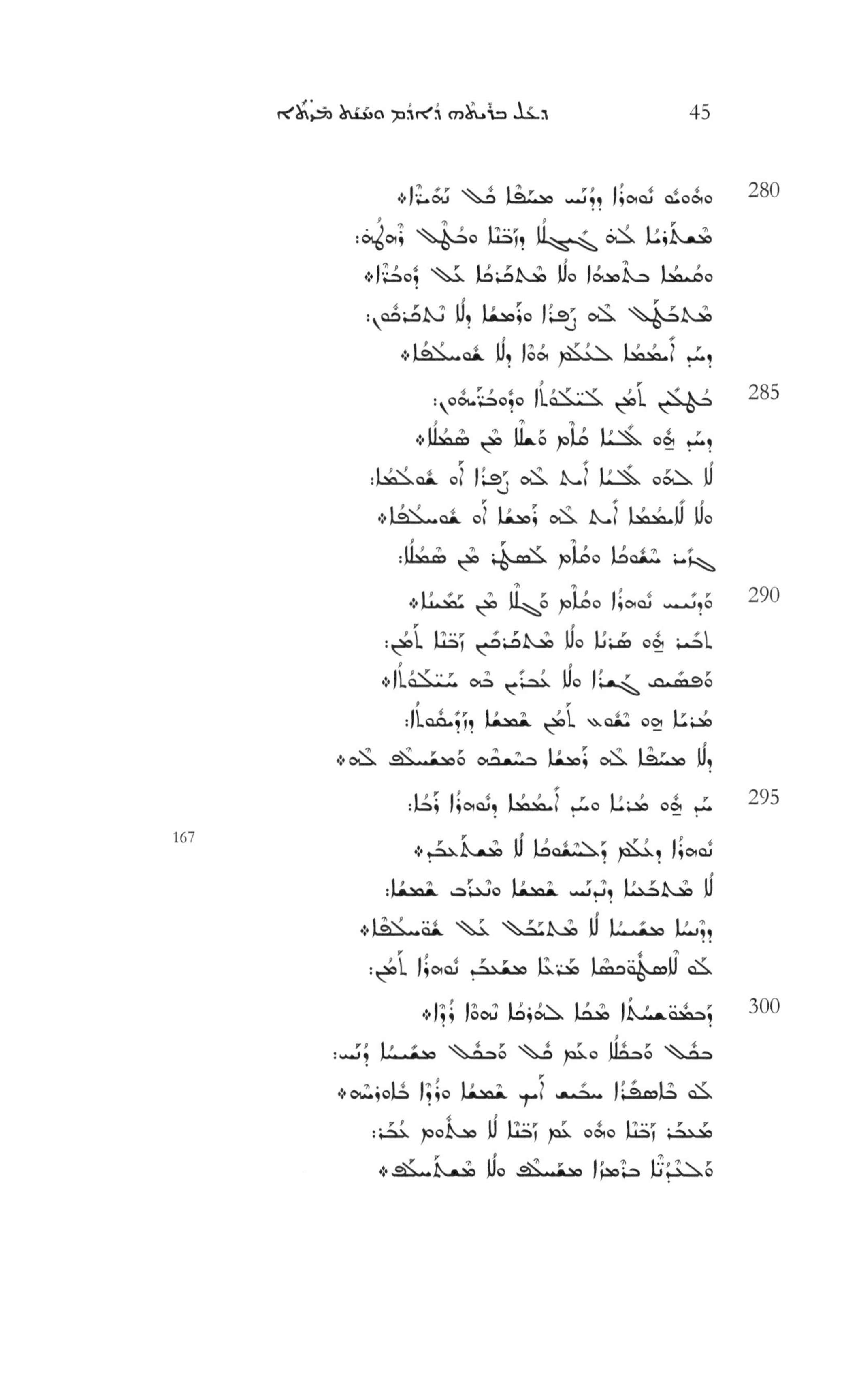

305	The course of all those things that are yoked comes to an end,
	they do not go about in their forms or at their times.
	Each one of the elements exists by itself,
	and that turbulence that is joined to their courses becomes silent.
	When that One separated the hot from the cold,
310	there was no course that could go beyond its functions.
	And when He separated the moist from the dry,
	there will no longer be any means for increase or for decrease.
	That very Will that mixed them now separated them,
	loosed them, brought them to an end, and restrained them.
315	Just like [man] the microcosm[47], He will dissolve the entire world,
	for the world and man are two worlds to the understanding.

VIII. THE END OF THE WORLD IS DEATH AND DISSOLUTION

	The dissolution of the world truly resembles a human death,
	and that death is a dissolution as well as an end.
	When a man dies his beautiful features fall off;
320	this makes clear how the beauties of the entire world come to an end.
	Your beloved is dead and his death has become like a teacher to you
	about how the entire world passes away from its beloved.
	The dome with its beauty and the lights that are arranged on it
	is wholly similar to the face of a man to one who looks upon it.
325	Just as when the beauty of the face is destroyed it likewise withers,
	so too is that dome destroyed at that final moment.
	The sun and the moon like beautiful pupils
	become dark at death and the dome is deprived of its lights.
	There are no eyes in the skull of a dead man when it decays,

---

[47] Jacob considers man as a microcosm in several places; see Jacob's "Homily on the Fifth Day of Creation"; Bedjan, III.88, also "Homily Two on the Last Judgement", V.858–861, and further references in Alwan, "L'homme, le «microcosme» selon Jacques de Saroug". This notion too has Jewish roots, see L. Ginzberg, *The Legends of the Jews*, I.49–50.

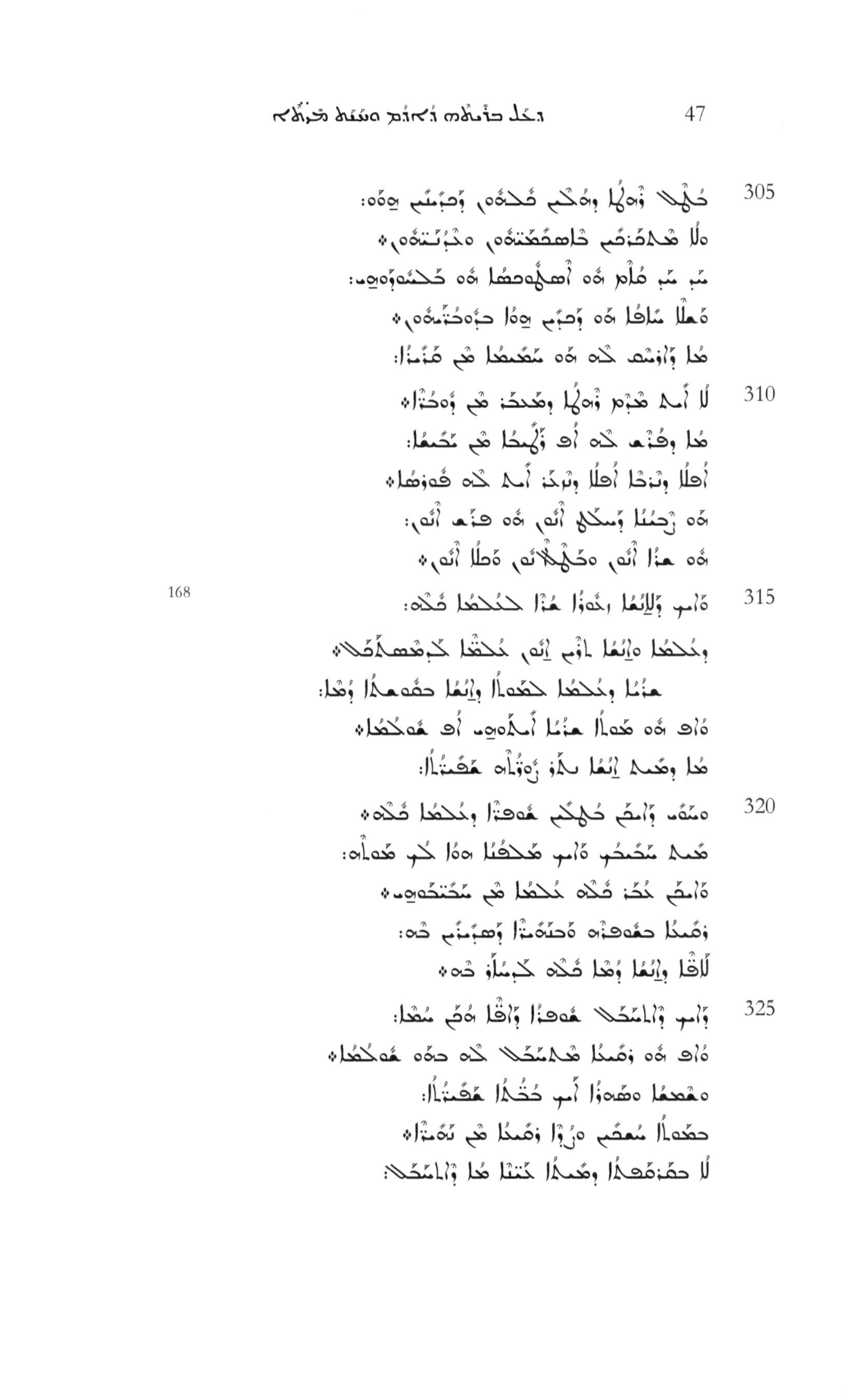

330 nor are the sun and the moon on the dome at that final moment.
A man dies and becomes a teacher to his companions,
just as the beauty of the world fades away when it reaches its end.
A creature when it is dissolved of its composition resembles
the body of a man when it is deprived of its limbs.
335 Look upon a corpse when it becomes corrupted in Sheol,
and look upon a creature when it decomposes and comes to its final end.
Death enters into the limbs of man in Sheol,
it disperses, dissipates, ruins and destroys their compositions.
So too does it happen to the world on the day of [its] end,
340 it bends down and falls, comes to an end and vanishes as if it had never existed.
Man too is constructed from the elements of the world,
and in his construction he is a world as we have said.[48]
So also at his death, when he is destroyed,
he is like the world when he draws his last breath.
345 Indeed, the death of one man is a type
of that end that comes to the world at the end of time.
Likewise both its functions and its courses come to an end,
as do the orders and the cycles of the world when it comes to its end.
The dissolution of the world first becomes clear to you at the death of your brother,
350 that when he passes away, your soul will not hold him in love.
Vision of the time that gives opportunity for repentance,
makes clear that at death the soul will reflect on that end.
Do not be led astray by this desirable world that will be destroyed,
and whose beauties will fall away and the force of whose delights will come to an end.

---

[48] See line 316, above.

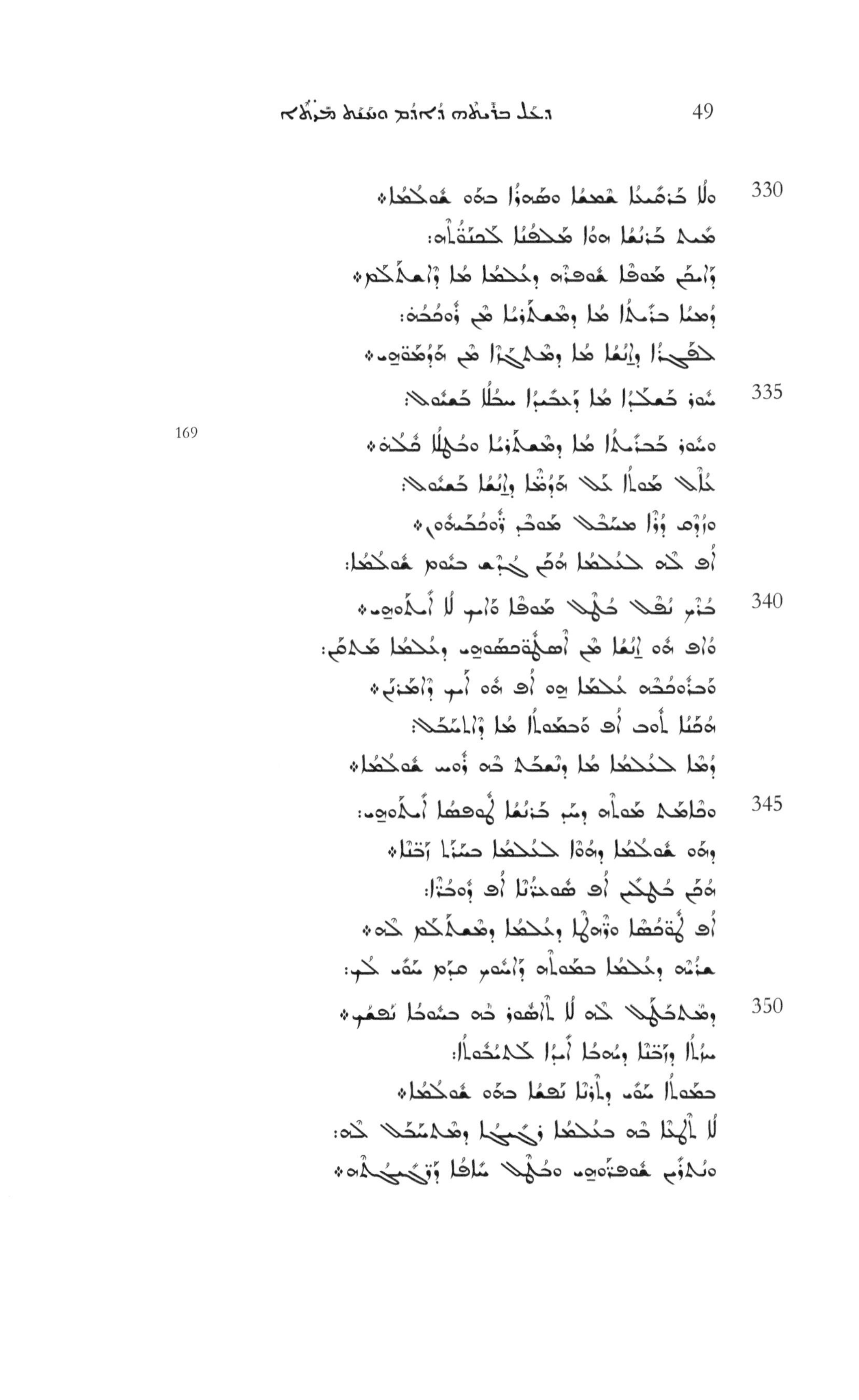

IX. AN EXHORTATION TO FORSAKE TEMPORAL THINGS AND LOOK TO THE ETERNAL

355 Woe to you, O soul, who loved the world and became a slave to it,
remove [your] hand from [its] delights for they will not endure.
Break off the shackles and chains and flee from the false one,
before he falls and by his fall he causes you to fall as well.
O comely soul whom the world has bound to its desires,
360 look upon this dead one for he too was desirable but is now destroyed.
Consider, O soul, the renewal that fire can bring about,
and renew[49] yourself before the flame overcomes you.
In the delightful waters of repentance restore your person,
before it comes and puts burning coals on your sores.
365 With the flowing of gentle tears heal your abscesses,
for they heal there in the flame — tremble before the fire.
If the pain makes you tremble then bandage it with repentance,
before the sea of fire roars and the world trembles.
Lo, a dead one has become a mirror for you, O discerning one,
370 look upon him and see that the world and its adornments pass away.
Reform yourself by it and repent from evil deeds,
look upon the dissolution of the world and how its beauty fades.
Give glory to that hidden power by which are joined
both worlds and men and at which they tremble yet [in which] they exist.
375 At its signal the [heavenly] hosts hasten along their paths,
and when it is pleased their functions and operations come to an end.

---

[49] Bedjan, III.170, here reads *ḥzy*, "see", but notes, n.5, the variant *ḥdty*, "renew", which fits the context here much better; Alwan IV.376, translates "renouvelle-toi", but with no mention of any variant.

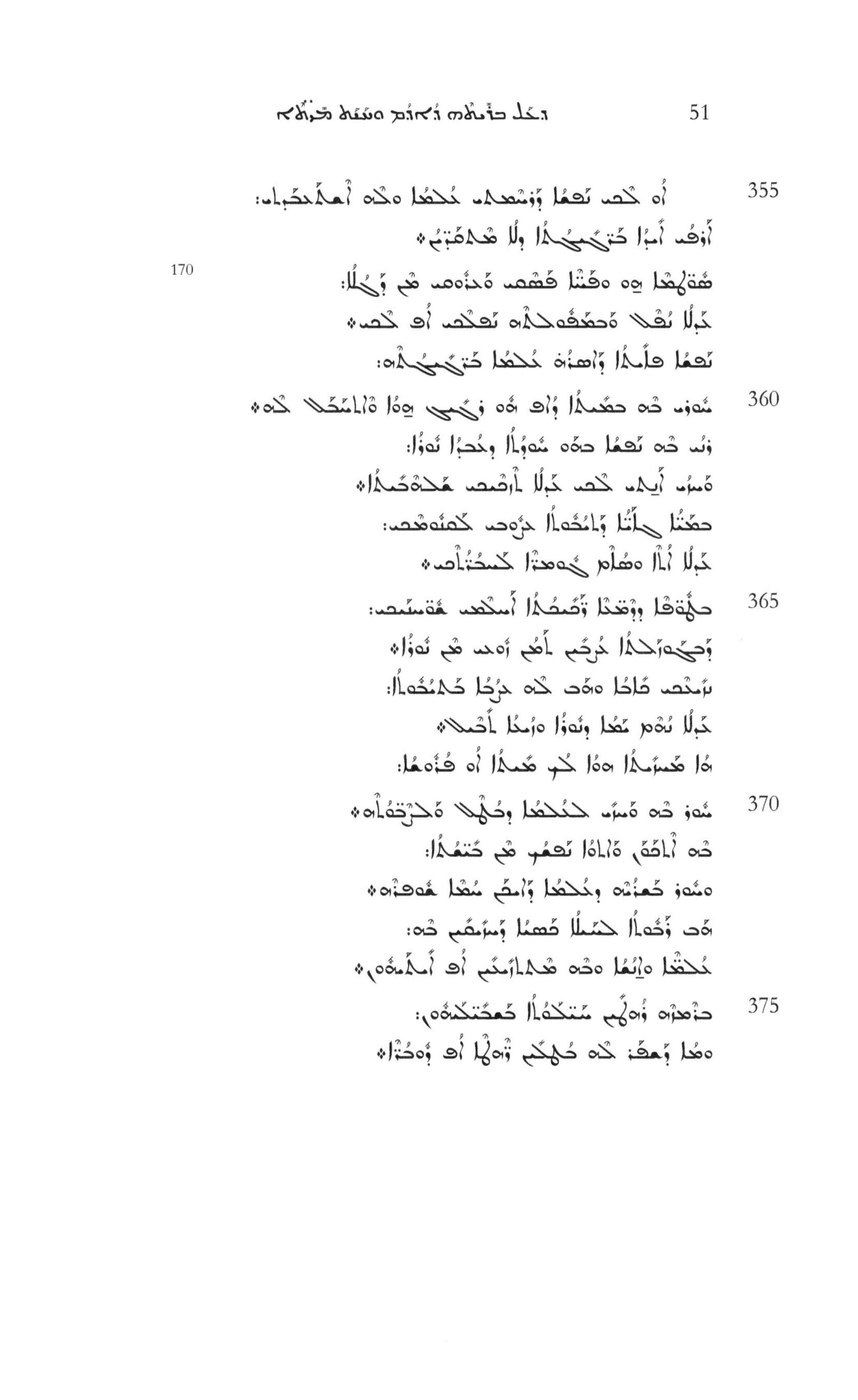

It unbinds them from their composition so that they no longer revolve,
and it binds up bodies lest they be handed over to corruption.

X. Adam Will Rise Up Again at the General Resurrection

The world is falling but Adam is rising from his fall,
380   that he might inherit the treasure prepared for him from the beginning.
A great and thunderous voice, continuous and persistent,
who with one signal has yoked both beginning and end.
With one command there will be a resurrection as well as the fall,
creation will fall and Adam will rise just as we have said.
385   At that signal by which all creation is dissolved,
the body of man will be girt with life that it may rise.
It is a voice that raises up and throws down, binds and looses,
that destroys and constructs, loosens and completes, though it does not toil.
It raises up the buried yet throws down and undoes all rulers.
390   It binds up bodies and dissolves the course of hosts.
It renews beauties and reconstructs His image which was destroyed,
in bringing the world to completion and to its restoration His signal initiates it.
The trembling is dreadful, the time is fearful and the voice is grievous,
resurrection is glorious and its story is beyond speech.
395   The sound of the resurrection reconstructs bones and breaks bodies,
it binds bodies and raises up the dead with great glory.
It uproots Sheol, binds up death, looses Adam,
rends rocks, opens graves, and raises up the dead.
Its voice is powerful, its strength is enormous, its signal swift,

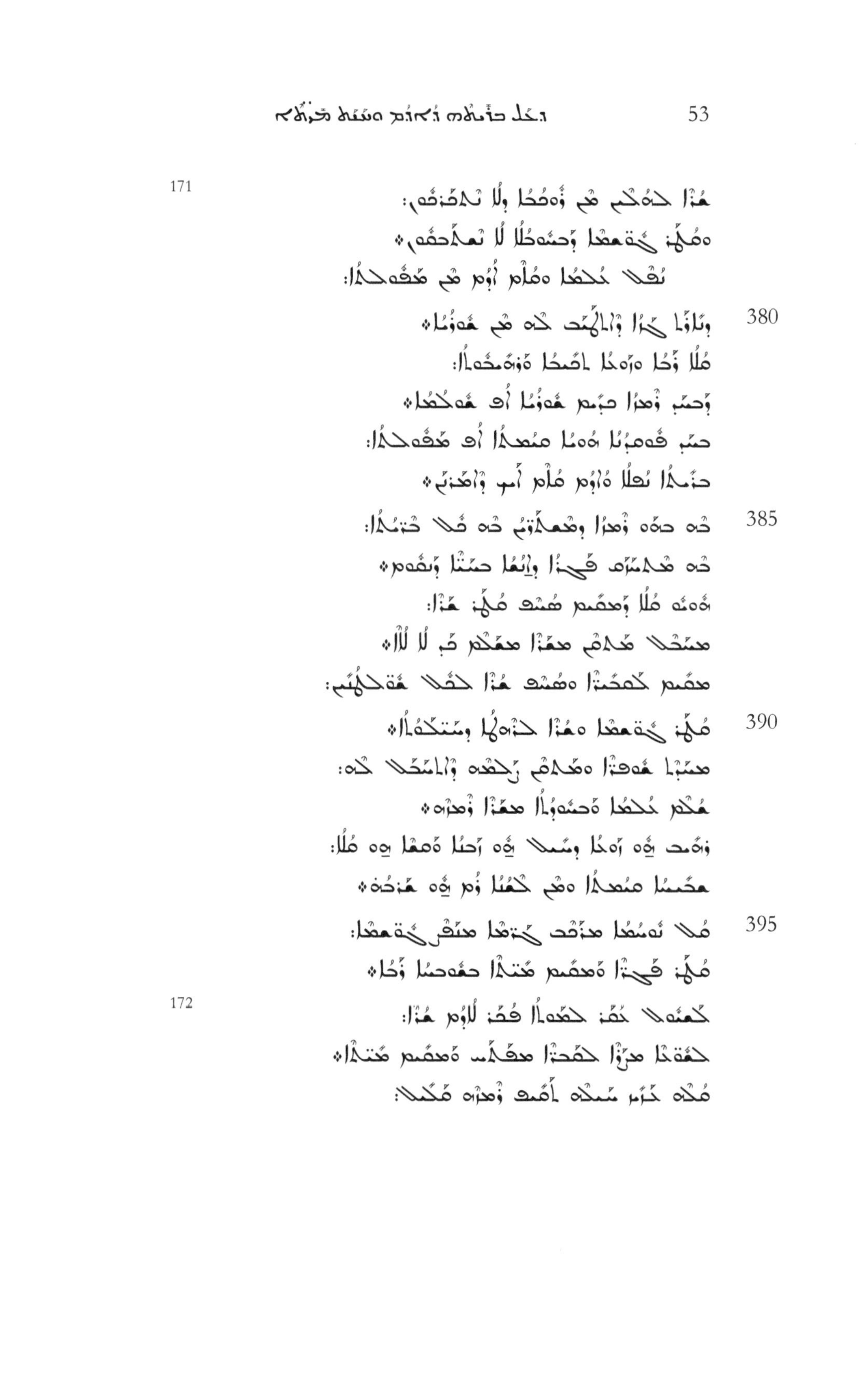

171

400   its word is great and by its will it will restore everything.
In wonder they will rise up, in glory and without corruption they
     will come
from destruction at the living signal of Him who is all-powerful.
The four that fell together will arise as one,
for neither beginning nor end shall ever again come upon them.
405   From the elements, one element will become a body,
which the resurrection will renew so that it might become immortal.
Four shall rise though they are one spiritually,
for there is no way for only one thing to be loosed.
Although they are one, they are from many,
410   for one will neither fall nor be changed because it is one.
As from a fiery furnace they shall come forth at the resurrection,
the four as one in an indestructible perfection.
All these honorable things that belong to nature
remain in the grave and the body arises without corruption.
415   The five senses that have fallen with it will rise with it,
not within any limit, but on a spiritual course.
He sees with them all, hears with them all, senses with them all,
tastes with them all and smells with them all, when he has been resurrected.

XI. The Spiritual Nature of the New Creation

In the new world, the body will move in spiritual fashion,
420   for like a spirit it will pass through even solid natures.
It will be easy for it to descend and to explore deep regions without
     effort,
and to go up and reach the top of high places without falling.
It will direct its own path before itself and pass through everything,
closed gates do not hinder it from entering into them.

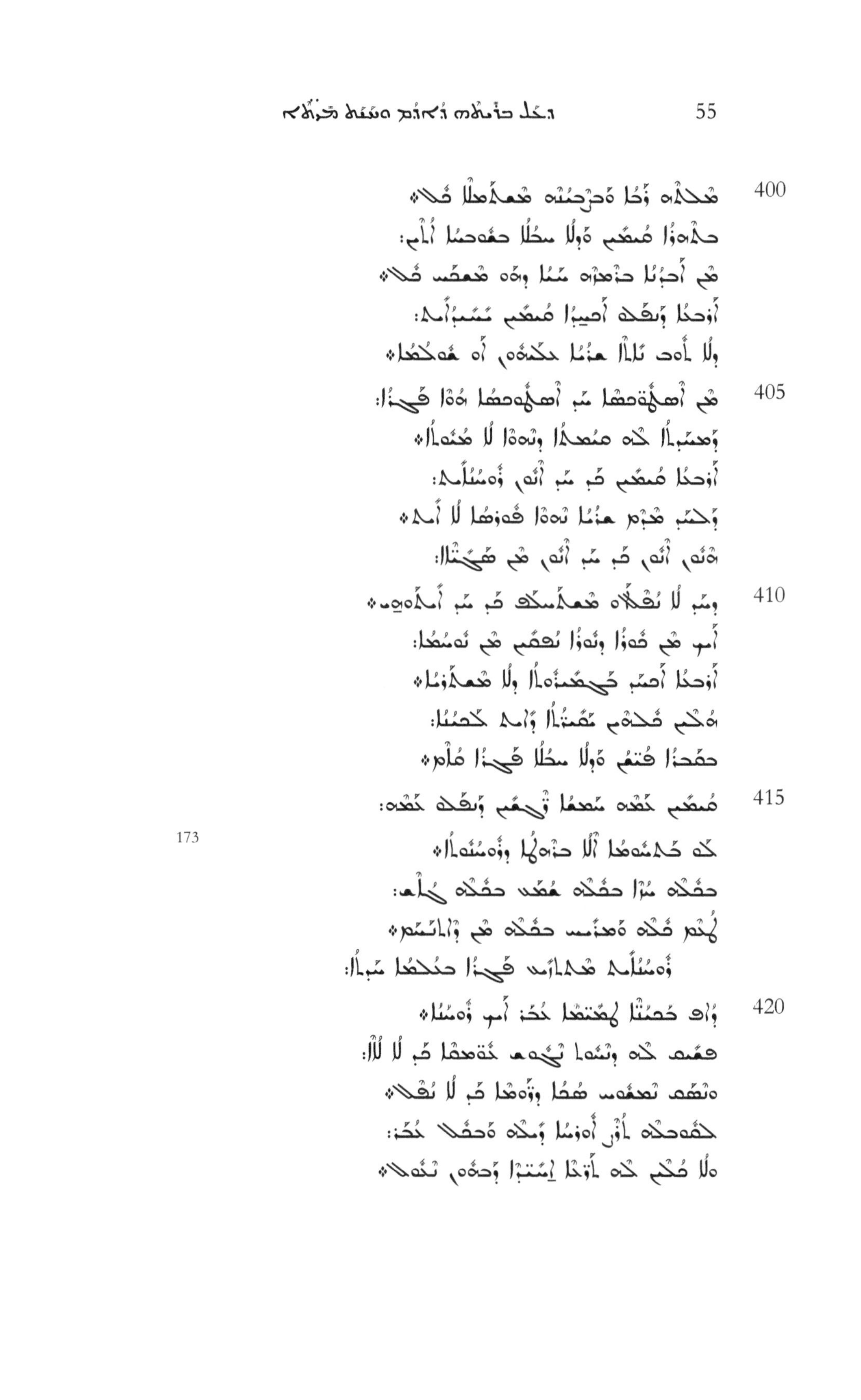

173

425 It is crowned and glittering, delicate and refined, perfect and polished,
and clothed in light in a world of light like an angel.
No anger or desire, hunger or thirst, laziness,
toil or sleep, disease or any sort of oppression,
Not one of these things will touch it once it is resurrected,
430 for it will be purified and will become a new, spiritual being.
At the resurrection the body will rise as a new creation,
as it will no longer be subservient to weakness or to change.
That signal, which gave it its nature from nothing, will dawn
and will perfect it that it may rise and become impassible.
435 Even though its limbs will rise up together with their components,
it will move entirely in a spiritual manner with no density.
It will acquire a completely ethereal and spiritual nature,
and it will cast aside all its corporeal movements.

XII. THE SAME ADAM WILL RISE UP AND REGAIN HIS GARMENT OF LIGHT

This body that fell and will rise up spiritually,
440 is nothing other than the same one that the serpent harmed.
It became naked but will be [re-]covered in a garment of glory,
that when it rises up its enemy might be shamed by the mercy that spared it.
For the one that fell it is a good thing that there be a resurrection,
for had he not fallen no resurrection would have been required.
445 The one who fell will rise up; for one who has not fallen there is no need to rise,
one who is dead will live but one who is not dead will not be resurrected.
This body which had stood naked in the garden,
will be clothed in glory and will be radiant at the resurrection.
To it belongs resurrection and to it belongs judgement by Justice;

425	
	:
	:
430	
	:
	:
435	:
	:
	:
440	
	:
445	:
	:
	:

450   it is right that it be victorious but not right that it be punished.
It will be raised up, it will be renewed, it will be praised,
it will be culpable, to it belongs both fire and the kingdom.
In wonder it shall arise, in splendor it shall shine, in glory it shall reign,
Blessed is He who renewed the image of Adam that had been corrupted.
The end of [the Homily] *On the Creation of Adam*

ܘܡܿܩܒܿܠ ܢܪ̈ܣܝ ܕܘܼܠܐ ܡܿܩܒܿܠ ܗ̱ܘܿ ܡܿܕܐܝܼܟܼܝ܂
ܗ̱ܘܿ ܡܿܕܐܝܼܣܹܡ ܗ̱ܘܿ ܡܿܕܐܝܼܣܒܵܐ ܗ̱ܘܿ ܡܿܕܐܡܿܟܼܒܼ܂
ܘܗ̱ܘܿ ܡܿܕܐܟܼܝܼܢܵܐ ܕܼܿܡܟܼܗ ܢܼܘܿܐ ܐܼܟܼ ܡܿܕܟܼܗܵܐܐ܂
ܒܐܬܼܘܿܐ ܚܿܐܡ ܕܼܿܢܼܐ ܡܿܚܿܢܹܝ ܚܿܦܘܼܚܣܿܐ ܡܿܚܿܣܟܼܝ܂
ܒܢܼܣܼܘ ܗܿ̇ܘ ܘܣܹܒܼܐ ܪܼܿܚܩܼܗ ܘܿܐܼܘܿܡ ܘܿܐܼܿܡܿܣܟܼܠܵܐ ܘܼܗܿܐ܂
ܥܒܼܝܼܡ ܘܟܼܠܵܐ ܕܼܿܢܼܡܸܗ ܘܿܐܼܘܿܡ.

BIBLIOGRAPHY OF WORKS CITED

PRIMARY TEXTS

Ephrem

Tonneau, Raymond M., ed. *Sancti Ephraem Syri in Genesim et in Exodum commentarii.* CSCO 152–53. Louvain: Peeters, 1955. Eng. trans. by Edward G. Mathews, Jr. in Edward G. Mathews, Jr. and Joseph P. Amar, *St. Ephrem the Syrian: Selected Prose Works.* Fathers of the Church, 91; Washington: Catholic University of America Press, 1994. Pp. 67–213.

Beck, Edmund, OSB, ed., *Des Heiligen Ephraem des Syrers Hymnen de Paradiso und Contra Julianum.* CSCO 174–175. Louvain: Peeters, 1957. Eng. trans. in Sebastian Brock, *St. Ephrem the Syrian: Hymns on Paradise.* Crestwood: St. Vladimir's Seminary Press, 1998.

Gregory of Nyssa

Smets, Alexis and Michel Van Esbroeck, eds. and trs., *Sur l'origine de l'homme. Hom. X et XI de l'Hexaéméron par Basile de Césarée.* Sources chrétiennes, 160. Paris: Éditions du Cerf, 1970.

De Opificio Hominis. PG 44, pp. 124–256. Eng. trans. in H.A. Wilson, tr., "Gregory of Nyssa: On the Making of Man." *A Select Library of Nicene and Post Nicene Fathers. Series Two.* Grand Rapids: Eerdmans, 1954. Vol. 5, pp. 387–427.

Isaac [of Antioch]

Bedjan, Paulus, ed., *Homiliae S. Isaaci Syri Antiocheni I.* Paris and Leipzig: Harrassowitz, 1903.

Unedited "Homily on Adam and Eve." In Ms. Vat. Syr. 120, ff. 154r–172r.

Jacob of Sarug

Alwan, Khalil, ed., *Jacques de Saroug, Quatre Homélies métriques sur la création*. 2 vols.; CSCO 509–510; Louvain, 1989.

Bedjan, Paulus, ed., with additional material by Sebastian P. Brock. *Homilies of Mar Jacob of Sarug*. 6 vols.; Piscataway: Gorgias Press, 2006 [original publication *Homiliae Selectae Mar-Jacobi Sarugensis*. 5 vols. Paris and Leipzig: Harrassowitz, 1905–1910].

Holy Transfiguration Monastery. "A Homily on the Giving of Praise for the Morning and Evening by Mar Jacob, Bishop of Serugh (†521)." *The True Vine* 7 (1998), 59–64.

Kollamparampil, Thomas. *Jacob of Sarug's Homily on Epiphany*. Texts from Christian Late Antiquity, 4. The Metrical Homilies of Mar Jacob of Sarug, 2; Piscataway: Gorgias Press, 2008.

Kollamparampil, Thomas. *Jacob of Sarug's Homily on Palm Sunday*. Texts from Christian Late Antiquity, 5. The Metrical Homilies of Mar Jacob of Sarug, 3; Piscataway: Gorgias Press, 2008.

Kollamparampil, Thomas. *Jacob of Sarug's Homilies on the Nativity*. Texts from Christian Late Antiquity, 23. The Metrical Homilies of Mar Jacob of Sarug, 18–20; Piscataway: Gorgias Press, 2010.

Mathews, Edward G., Jr. *Jacob of Sarug's Homilies on the Six Days of Creation: The First Day*. Texts from Christian Late Antiquity, 27; Metrical Homilies of Mar Jacob of Sarug, 29. Piscataway: Gorgias Press, 2009.

Narsai

Gignoux, Philippe. *Homélies de Narsaï sur la création*. Patrologia Orientalis, 34.3–4 [161–162]. Turnhout: Brepols, 1968.

Theodore of Mopsuestia

McLeod, Frederick G. *Theodore of Mopsuestia*. Early Church Fathers. London and New York: Routledge, 2009.

SECONDARY WORKS

Alwan, Khalil. "L'homme, le «microcosme» selon Jacques de Saroug." *Parole de l'Orient* 13 (1986), 51–78.

Alwan, Khalil. "Le 'remzo' selon la pensée de Jacques de Saroug." *Parole de l'Orient* 15 (1988–1989), 91–106.

Alwan, Khalil. "L'homme était-il mortel ou immortel avant le péché, pour Jacques de Saroug." *Orientalia Christiana Periodica* 55 (1989), 5–31.
Becker, Adam H. *Fear of God and the Beginning of Wisdom: The School of Nisibis and the Development of Scholastic Culture in Late Antique Mesopotamia*. Philadelphia: University of Pennsylvania Press, 2006.
Bou Mansour, Tanios. *La théologie de Jacques de Saroug. Tome I: Création, Anthropologie, Ecclésiologie et Sacraments*. Bibliothèque de l'Université Saint-Esprit, 36; Kaslik: l'Université Saint-Esprit, 1993.
Bouteneff, Peter C. *Beginnings: Ancient Christian Readings of the Biblical Creation Narratives*. Grand Rapids: Baker Academic, 2008.
Brock, Sebastian P. "Clothing Metaphors as a Means of Theological Expression in Syriac Tradition." In Margot Schmidt, ed., *Typus, Symbol, Allegorie bei den östlichen Vatern und ihren Parallelen im Mittelalter*. Eichstätt, 1981. Pp. 11–40. Reprinted in idem, *Studies in Syriac Christianity* (Variorum Reprints, 1992, chapter XI).
Brock, Sebastian P. *The Luminous Eye: The Spiritual World Vision of St. Ephrem*. Rome: CIIS, 1985. 2d ed., *CSS* 124. Kalamazoo: Cistercian Publications, 1992.
Jansma, Taeke. "L'Hexaméron de Jacques de Sarug." *L'Orient Syrien* 4 (1959), 3–42, 129–162, 253–284.
Kollamparampil, Thomas. "Adam-Christ Complementar[it]y and the Economy of Salvation in Jacob of Serugh." *The Harp* 13 (2000), 147–170.
Kollamparampil, Thomas. *Salvation in Christ according to Jacob of Serugh: An Exegetico-theologival Study on the Homelies of Jacob of Serugh (451–521 AD) on the Feasts of Our Lord*. Early Syriac Christian Patristic Studies. Bangalore: Dharmaram Publications, 2001.
Kronholm, Tryggve. *Motifs from Genesis 1–11 in the Genuine Hymns of Ephrem the Syrian with particular reference to the influence of Jewish exegetical tradition*. Coniectanea Biblica. Old Testament Series, 11. Uppsala: Almqvist & Wiksell, 1978.
Levinson, John R. *Portraits of Adam in Early Judaism: From Sirach to 2 Baruch*. Journal for the Study of Pseudopigrapha Supplement Series, 1. Sheffield: JSOT Press, 1988.

Louth, Andrew, ed. *Genesis 1–11*. Ancient Christian Commentary on Scripture. Old Testament, 1. Downers Grove: InterVarsity Press, 2001.

Mathews, Edward G., Jr. "Isaac of Antioch and the Literature of Adam and Eve." In Esther G. Chazon, David Satran, and Ruth A. Clements, eds., *Things Revealed: Studies in Early Jewish and Christian Literature in Honor of Michael E. Stone*. Supplements to the Journal for the Study of Judaism, 89. Leiden: E.J. Brill, 2004. Pp. 331–344.

Mathews, Edward G., Jr. "'What Manner of Man?': Early Syriac Reflections on Adam." In Robert D. Miller, ed., *Syriac and Antiochian Exegesis and Biblical Theology for the 3rd Millennium*. Gorgias Eastern Christian Studies, 6. Piscataway: Gorgias Press, 2008. Pp. 115–149.

Russell, Jeffrey Burton. *The Devil: Perceptions of Evil from Antiquity to Primitive Christianity*. Ithaca: Cornell University Press, 1977.

Sony, Behnam M. Boulos. "La méthode exégétique de Jacques de Saroug." *Parole de l'Orient* 9 (1979–1980), 67–103.

Sony, Behnam M. Boulos. "Hymne sur la création de l'homme de l'hexaméron de Jacques de Saroug." *Parole de l'Orient* 11 (1983), 167–200.

Sony, Behnam M. Boulos. "L'anthropologie de Jacques de Saroug." *Parole de l'Orient* 12 (1984–1985), 153–185.

Van Rompay, Lucas. "Humanity's Sin in Paradise: Ephrem, Jacob of Serugh, and Narsai in Conversation." In George Anton Kiraz, ed., *Jacob of Serugh and His Times: Studies in Sixth-Century Syriac Christianity*. Gorgias Eastern Christian Studies, 8. Piscataway: Gorgias Press, 2010. Pp. 199–217.

INDEX

NAMES AND THEMES

Adam	1, 20, 26, 28, 41, 111, 159, 216, 217, 223, 227, 379, 384, 397, 454	Good One	5, 13
		Great King	64
		Honored one	191
		icon	62
Apostles	253	image	7, 11, 20, 21, 30, 51, 53, 55, 63, 64, 65, 69, 76, 138, 154, 157, 189, 193, 194, 205, 234, 391, 454
beauty	17, 20, 33, 59, 64, 88, 95, 103, 104, 110, 111, 112, 144, 149, 156, 184, 188, 218, 320, 323, 325, 332, 354, 372, 391		
		Jesus	293
		Jeweler	113
		Judge	254
bridal chamber	158, 167	Just One	61
chamber of light	13	King	194, 247
Christ	279, 298, 301	Lord	11, 60, 62, 140, 171, 195, 217, 293, 295
Creator	3, 29, 39, 53, 139		
Divinity	189	Maker	151
dragon	105	Malicious one	175
Eden	5, 13, 167, 178	mercy	201, 202, 204, 222, 232, 442
Eve	159	Michael	251
Evil one	6, 14, 64	microcosm	315
Exalted One	7, 42	Most High	197
False one	357	Only-Begotten	206
Gabriel	249	Paul	251
garment of light	185, 441	Satan	12
God/god	3, 120, 223, 228	serpent	65, 141, 180, 185, 440

Sheol	14, 100, 106, 190, 335, 337, 397	Son of God	220, 228
		Son of the King	194, 255
		Sun of Righteousness	293
sign	238	tree of knowledge	91, 169, 172, 174, 181
signal	151, 240, 259, 304, 375, 382, 385, 392, 399, 402, 433	tree of life	167
		viper	109
		Wisdom	7, 11, 30, 42, 55, 57, 140
Simon	249		
sin	67	Wise One	28, 137

Biblical References

Gen 1:26	1, 7, 205	Zech 14:7	284
Gen 1:31	19	Mal 4:2	293
Gen 2:7	31, 152	Matt 18:12	196
Gen 2:9–10	40, 164	Matt 24:29	267
Gen 2:15	5	Mark 13:24	267
Gen 2:16–17	174	Luke 15:4	196
Gen 2:19–20	40	1 Cor 15:45	153
Gen 3:1–7	65	Eph 1:7	206, 228
Gen 3:3	60	1 Thess 4:16	207
Gen 3:6	181	2 Tim 4:1	256
Gen 3:7	186	1 Pet 1:18–19	206, 228
Ps 8:5-9	1	1 Pet 4:5	256
Ps 145(146):6	15	Apoc 21:23	261, 280
Isa 60:19	261	Apoc 22:5	280

www.ingramcontent.com/pod-product-compliance
Lightning Source LLC
Chambersburg PA
CBHW052029290426
44112CB00014B/2443